Praise

"Fantasy meets real[...] [...mem]oir, propelled by the [vivacious, utterly engaging voice of] our compulsively honest narrator. A real page-turner."

- Phillip Lopate

"Heather Siegel has an awesome sense of humor and a penetrating view of what contemporary marriage is all about. And as a newlywed, I was thrilled to read about all that's in store for me! This is a page-turning, laugh-out-loud tale of triumphant love, and self-love, and a cautionary story of both when to compromise and when never to give up or give in."

- Neesha Arter, author of *Controlled: The Worst Night of My Life* and *Its Aftermath*

"Heather Siegel's latest is a love story for the ages, but not in the way you think. While her vivid descriptions of falling for her soulmate make it impossible for the reader not to travel back in time to their first love, it's Siegel's keen insight that gives the reader the gift of watching her—a strong, independent, wits-about-her bad ass—fall back in love with herself. In a time where women's freedoms and choices are in danger, Heather Siegel takes back her power, her life, and her spirit in a true story of love, loss, and finding out who you really are. This is a must-read for anyone who's been looking for themselves, and everyone who has never thought they had to."

- Lauren J. Sharkey, *Inconvenient Daughter*

"[*The King & The Quirky*] is a powerful memoir of a process that will be familiar to many women: one which involves the remarkable task of reconsidering life's goals and possibilities within and beyond the traditions of marital bliss and connection... [Siegel's] memoir represents an important survey of both the evolution of hope and self and the end results of such pursuits, creating an accessible, humorous, involving account highly recommended for women at various stages of growth."

- Diane Donovan, *Midwest Book Review*

"With wit and insight, Heather Siegel offers a fresh look at an ancient institution. Leaving no cultural assumption unturned, she illustrates how marriage can be a clarifying crucible for the bravest of us, pushing us to encounter each other in all our complexity, and making us the better for it."

- Rebecca Baum, author of *Lifelike Creatures*

"Heather Siegel does the rarest of things: she speaks the truth about marriage with warmth, wit and lacerating self-awareness. With an uncanny eye for detail, Siegel teaches powerful lessons that should be required learning for anyone in love: Chemistry and compatibility are not the same. The first few months of your relationship bears little resemblance to the next 40 years. You can't change your partner but if you can accept each other's flaws and repeatedly choose kindness over resentment, you can create a happy life. *The King and The Quirky* is a singular accomplishment: a deeply personal story that is universal to any reader who has ever been married."

- Evan Katz, dating coach and author of four books, including *Believe in Love*

"Heather Siegel takes a deep dive into matrimony and motherhood… Witty, big-hearted, and brutally honest, Siegel keeps us engaged as she takes us through her trials and tribulations, heroically evolving into a person of her own—all the while questioning conventional notions of love and happiness. An inspirational and memorable read."

- Esther Amini, author of *Concealed: A Memoir of a Jewish/Iranian Daughter Caught Between the Chador and America.*

THE KING AND *the Quirky*

A Memoir of Love, Marriage, Domesticity, Feminism, and Self

Heather Siegel

Regal House Publishing

Published by
Regal House Publishing, LLC
Raleigh, NC 27612
All rights reserved

ISBN -13 (paperback): 9781947548954
ISBN -13 (epub): 9781646030224
Library of Congress Control Number: 2019941546

Interior and cover design by Lafayette & Greene
lafayetteandgreene.com
Cover images © by Marchie/Shutterstock

Regal House Publishing, LLC
https://regalhousepublishing.com

Printed in the United States of America

To the one and only Jon,
the incomparable Jules, and my ever-evolving tribe,
without whom none of this would be as much fun.

"There is nowhere like Long Island."
- *T.B., Dix Hills, married twelve years*

"Long Island is pretty typical of U.S. Suburbia."
- *J.G., Oyster Bay, married nine years*

Intro

I used to feel bad about killing the mice. Ten years ago, I would cup spiders, even mosquitoes, and free them outside. Once, I saw a squirrel get clipped by a car—his little gray body hurtled from street to sidewalk. I swerved to the side of the road and rigged a stretcher from an old Gap T-shirt and manila folder containing tax documents. I scooped up the terrified animal, slid him into the bushes, and covered him from the neck down with my T-shirt.

"Sorry, little guy. I'm just so sorry." I blinked back the tears, trying not to ruin my edgy black liner; they came anyway, and I cried for his pain as well as the injustice of mankind's selfish need for more roads. After finishing my errands, I returned to check on him. He was gone. Had I saved his life?

I liked to think so.

"Either that or you gift-wrapped a meal for a hawk," my husband said when I told him the story ten years later. We were setting down mouse traps in our farmhouse kitchen. My cats, who had kept the mice at bay for years, had died of old age by then, and we were now reliant on Ace Hardware to ward off little black droppings.

I hadn't gone straight for the snap-and-kill devices my husband had left under the sink. "For when you're ready to get real," he'd said. Instead, I'd held my ground and tried the sonic plug-ins and the spearmint pouches that looked like oversize tea bags. But eventually droppings sprinkled the floor around the stove, peppered the insides of cabinets and drawers, and littered the bottom pantry shelf.

1

I didn't want to get real, and I sure as hell didn't want to concede. But vaguely aware that the droppings were a metaphor for all I could no longer control in my life, and possibly even for the gazillion resentments I clung to, I reached under the sink, smeared peanut butter onto the yellow plastic faux cheese bits, and hoped for a small victory.

Still, it was shocking that first time I found the innocent creature served up on that little wooden board, eyes bulging, head hooked in place. I felt terrible. Did he really deserve this cruel death?

The second time, I felt a little more pragmatic about it. Mice did carry disease, and I had a child to worry about now. By the third mouse, I'd developed a utilitarian stoicism. I mean, what had to be done, had to be done. But I'd be lying if I didn't admit that, every now and then, I felt a touch of sadistic satisfaction as I dropped the trap into the garbage pail.

"I warned, you, motherfucker," I actually whispered aloud one morning. And that's when it hit me. Marriage can really change a person. Which isn't necessarily a bad thing, in and of itself. Unless, of course, you realize you don't actually like the person you've become and want to get back to your old self but don't know how.

Then what?

Well, first, you recognize you're not alone, understanding this metamorphosis can happen to the best of us, to women who once lit pathways for themselves, who commanded their careers and listened to their dreams, or, at the least, to those women who once operated as independent beings in the world before they entrapped themselves in marital bliss (or as I like to call it on a bad day, the identity-sucking vortex of domestic life).

Second, I suppose you do what you do when you've lost anything—say, your keys. You retrace your steps to where you last saw them.

"It's hard to believe there is only one person for you in the entire world."

- *A.H., Huntington, married thirteen years*

GRANOLA GIRL

I was handling things all by my grown-up, thirty-four-year-old self. Frothing milk with one hand, I spurted chocolate sauce onto a floating pile of homemade whipped cream and spun around to expedite a tray of steamed, sugary concoctions.

"Order up!" I tapped the bell, the kind found on the counter of an old-fashioned reception desk. The nearest employee, Ronan, a freckled computer engineer with milky skin, a red afro, and Pavlovian reflexes, whisked off the tray in time for Jen, a modern dancer with a swinging black ponytail, to pirouette toward the next one landing down.

But no matter how nimbly, on this or any given Saturday night, we served the eighty or so guests crammed onto velvet couches, tufted ottomans, and precarious chairs purchased from the Salvation Army, which could snap and break at any given moment, no matter how loudly we called to one another—*table three still waiting on a Turkey Zest! table fourteen needs their Oreo Granita*—it all felt at the time like a dream in which we couldn't run fast enough.

And for ten years, I'd loved every second of it.

"Table nine's staring," I informed Craig, a twenty-two-year-old "triple threat" with purple-tipped hair, ginger skin, and an outgoing personality he hoped would land him a part in Broadway's *Rent*.

"On it." He loaded his arms with plates and disappeared into the mayhem. I beamed, proud of his multi-tasking abilities, proud of the whole staff. Since the inception of the coffeehouse, I'd rarely had to fire anyone; the place did it for me. You either had the ability to remain calm and steady as people swarmed this cozy 1400-square-foot space—threatening

3

to knock over your teetering trays, while the folk musician's jacked-up volume rattled the windows and mirrors, the blenders and steamers roared, and the hostess yelled into the makeshift microphone of her cupped hand, trying to keep track of the names in her notebook and the made-up times she'd told them (*half hour wait, one hour wait, an hour and a half wait*), because there was really no way of knowing who was here for the dessert, music, after-movie treat, or night out—or you didn't.

Logically, there seemed no good reason why that little store with its giant wooden coffee cup for a sign, mismatched couches, red velvet drapes, vintage candle holders, and sun-flower and orange walls covered in pieces by local artists—a place I was told time and again seemed transported from Williamsburg, Manhattan, or San Francisco—should have done well, smack in the center of working class Long Island suburbia. Especially in the town of Wantagh, known for an Irish-Catholic crowd, pubs, diners, churches, and houses dec-orated in Victorian dark wood paneling and traditional-style furniture. Nor did it seem obvious why Wednesday's Open Mic was standing room only, why Psychic Night would book weeks in advance, or why the place would garner a reputation in the local press and media as a destination nightlife spot, drawing people from all walks of life, ages, ethnicity, sexual orientation, and towns.

Except maybe to me, that independent being, operating not only in the world but who also trusted instinct to guide her. To that person, everything about the place made sense, beginning with the fact that I bet on the contrarian theory: Long Island had no place like it and that meant no com-petition. Besides, I'd reasoned, why should Williamsburg or Manhattan or San Francisco have all the fun anyway?

Also, I cared about every square inch of the place, which, as any small business owner knows, creates a good portion of the magic. Every angle of every sequined or furry throw pillow needed to be just so, every corner scrubbed, every deck of cards returned to its pack, every syrup bottle polished with its label facing outward, every tea infuser and spoon sterilized clean and shiny, every dessert decorated in an approved design of geometric patterns and flowers using plastic-tipped bottles of chocolate, orange, white chocolate, and berry elixirs. Now and then, when an employee went rogue and created, say, a toothpick stenciling of a human profile, she knew to come to me first for approval.

Somewhere along the way, I'd surmised that people wanted to be entertained when they went out, or maybe I just needed that. But why look at bland lamp shades when you could read quotes on them, scribbled in fabric marker? *And the trouble is, if you don't risk anything, you risk even more.—Erica Jong.* Why order mundane things like hot chocolate and coffee, when you could instead order Hot Mocha Cocoa and The Third Rail? Why read off the backs of the employees' T-shirts something pedestrian like Staff when, instead, you could read the motto, *Liquefy the Soul,* which no one understood, including the owner and the employee who came up with it.

Not that this last point mattered. The employees always had an excuse for why they forgot to wear their shirts, and I was okay with that, knowing the real reason was because they wanted to show off their personal style, which also contributed to the place's charisma.

Yes, it all made perfect sense to me inside my insular little bubble. It was life *outside*, that alien world of mainstream Long Island suburbia, I couldn't understand. In-laws, soccer championships, parent-teacher conferences: a life that moved with the flow of the stream instead of against it?

Boring!

Or so I told myself.

One particular Saturday night—sometime in October

2003—this ten-year streak of mine would suffer an interruption. And what would come next I can't blame anyone for, except myself. And society. I can blame society, and poets, and painters, and fairy tales, and my friends, and magazines, and television print ads, and self-help classes, and spirituality, and the couple at the coffeehouse I'm about to describe, and my parents, and Obama. Kidding about Obama. He wasn't even elected yet, but he gets blamed for everything else, so why not? He and Michelle still make their love partnership seem like a one-in-seven-billion connection, which as much as anything, may have chipped away at my resistance.

"Heath, any chance you can bring this to table twelve?" Gia asked, scrunching the crescent of studs over each eyebrow she planned to take out once accepted to medical school. I scooped up the plate and headed for a twenty-something couple nuzzling each other on a gold velour loveseat.

"Brownie sundae?" I auctioned. Getting no answer, I set the dessert down along with two gleaming forks.

"It's beautiful," the girl said, tears in her eyes. She waved her newly minted hand to let the diamond catch the light from the hanging lamp above. Audrey Lorde was quoted on the lampshade: *Our visions begin with our desires.*

"Wow, congrats," I offered.

"You know, we actually met here," the guy said.

"Really? That's fantastic," I lied, my gut prickling. Neighboring people swarmed the couple, offering congrats. I edged back to slinging sugar and milk, the needling sensation continuing. But why? As I rang people up and blended drinks, I stole glances at the couple. Maybe I somehow felt complicit that another couple was swallowing the Kool-Aid, and I'd provided cups for sipping.

It was hard to take marriage seriously in this land of commercialized wedding factories, bridal shops, and Bridal Expos, especially at this age, when everyone was getting hitched—and un-hitched. *To finding your great love!* To meeting the one! To your everything! I would no sooner toast my champagne glass, when I'd have to open my couch for a friend transitioning back to her single self. *It's like we don't even know each other anymore.* Of course, some couples seemed to be doing *okay*, but I was hard-pressed to name one married person I knew, or even one person in a long-term relationship, who would still vouch for their "everything."

And here's where the tale really unraveled for me—that we could have an "everything." As I saw it, this meant having three intangible abstracts within one person, which I'd so far experienced in bits and pieces with different people at different times. These abstracts were: eroticism, romantic love, and companionship, all rolled into one person like a perfect burrito. How was that possible?

"It's not something you can define," friends would insist. "You'll just know." At twenty-four, I didn't know anything. At thirty, I knew even less. By thirty-four, I'd decided this love narrative I'd heard in one form or another my whole life through movies, literature, fairy tales, pop culture, even my own parents' story of how they met and "knew"—something my father would cling to even after my mother left us—was simply that. A narrative. Of fiction. One I was still encountering in a city MFA program I was finishing, rereading of all things *Romeo and Juliet*, the first love story to mention "star-crossed" lovers, two people fated to meet who are so in love that death is preferable to the alternative of living without each other. This seemed almost comical. If I didn't know one married person who half believed in her own narrative anymore, I sure as heck didn't know one who was willing to vouch for her significant other by drinking a vial of poison.

I whipped past another lampshade to seat a table of three. *Love is a construct, to make more of our biological selves than we are,* it read, with its attribution anonymous. I relished the secret knowledge that the source was me.

Floors mopped, cappuccino machine steam cleaned, I drove home at 2:30 a.m., enjoying the solitude of the road, the glow of the streetlights, the flickers of fluorescent lighting from strip mall shopping centers. The wind whipped through the windows of my Jetta, a warm, portent swirl in the weeks before Halloween, just before the cold moves in. I turned up the sounds of Ani Di Franco, belted along about virtues of marginalization, and pulled into my town of East Meadow, or "East Ghetto," as its own blue-collar residents had named it (my guess is on account of the many bars and 7-Elevens, though to be fair it had an equal number of worship houses and pizza/pasta places, too).

I wound onto my block, passing a six-foot-high inflated lawn spider with purple glowing eyes, and lowered the music so as not to disturb my neighbors. Their television lights were already extinguished in the bay windows of their Cape-style homes; their orange Halloween lights, covered with faux cobwebs, unplugged. But who knows how many of them still lay awake, these mostly married couples, privately hoping, as my ex-boyfriend and I had, that whatever this thing called love was, or whatever this "knowing" was, would grow on them like wisdom or fungus.

I parked in the driveway and went inside to run a bath, reminding myself I'd chosen authenticity, despite feeling rotten for initiating the breakup with my boyfriend and for needing to justify why. "But he's such a great catch!" friends puzzled. And he had been. An electrician with a great job and dark sculptural hair straight out of a Disney movie, he volunteered for Habitat for Humanity and made pasta for his mother on Sundays. But two years in, lying beside him in that pre-dawn stillness when the truth reveals itself, I began to understand I would never feel more than that companion side of the "everything" triangle with him. Worse, I could see into the future, thanks to a recurring dream, and knew I would continue to feel this way ten years in, only with a few kids in tow.

With the tub full, I stepped into scalding water, sure it was better to be alone than to be false, despite my friends' insistence that my "picky" attitude would one day lead me to an unhealthy relationship with knitting and cats (and besides that half of the prophecy had already materialized. I was fairly certain my black-and-white male cat had once been a curmudgeonly man who'd been demoted on account of bad behavior).

Being alone meant empowerment and freedom, I told myself, lowering my back against the porcelain. There was no one to complain to about eating braised tofu with walnut mushroom gravy for the third night in a row at my favorite vegetarian restaurant in the city; no one to make a peep about my seventy-two-hour writing binge, ending only when the chaos of words came to order; no one to resist my working twelve days in a row or taking raw foods classes, where I was learning to make cultured vegetables; no one to balk at my attending Kabbalah classes, where I was learning—or trying to learn, anyway—how to unlock the secrets to "The Game of Life."

I dipped underwater and closed my eyes. "I think therefore I am single," the comedian Lizz Winstead once said. As the heat enveloped my neck and the tension drained, I couldn't have agreed more. Save for that little pinprick in my belly.

I thought about what the rabbi had said about these little needlings during a recent class. He called them "alarms" and said it was important to pay attention to them. "They start off quiet and gentle, and when we don't heed them, they get louder and louder, until we can't hear anything else."

Had I really pitied the couple? Or…was I upset witnessing people seemingly moving forward in life, however faulty I believed their move was? Somewhere along the self-improvement path, I'd read about the natural cycle of renewal and growth—the idea being that we grow restless and need major change every ten years; that it's part of our destiny to keep moving. I was a late bloomer. It had taken me a third of my life to finally question why, besides having grown up in Long Island and having a best-friend-brother and best-friend-sister nearby, I'd not only set up shop but continued to root myself in this small sheltered parcel of Earth.

No doubt, Long Island had its claim to fame, with its bagels, delis, beaches and vineyards, with its artistic connections to old greats like Walt Whitman, Jackson Pollock, and F. Scott Fitzgerald, and newer greats like The Baldwin brothers, Howard Stern, and Billy Crystal. But it was also home to not so greats like Amy Fischer and Joey Buttafucco, notorious for its tanning and nail salons and weird accents, like "cawfee" for coffee and "Long Guyland" for Long Island. If Manhattanites looked down upon Brooklynites for their lack of New Yorkness, I think it's fair to say that most boroughs snubbed their noses at Long Islanders. Or maybe it was just me passing judgement. Or me wondering if I was trying too hard to create an oasis within. Or me knowing that there existed someplace on this planet more simpatico for me, culturally and geographically.

I didn't know then about something called a primal landscape—the idea that our physical surroundings in childhood inform our notion of place as adults and that the sage and heather and redwoods and pines and wide open spaces I'd experienced in the woods of Northern California where I was born, acted as a sort of baseline landscape, biasing me against the sixty by sixty orderly lots of land in East Meadow.

But I'd traveled enough to know there was a big wide world worth exploring beyond where I was, or suburbia for that matter, places where you didn't have to commute to find culture, where the single population was more than eighteen percent, where you could walk to reach your destination (imagine!), where you could pick up a gift for someone other than the intentionally designed "shopping trap" of a mall.

I drained the bath water, now lukewarm, and considered

taking another trip to scout out San Diego. Maybe it wasn't "home"—wherever that mysterious place on earth was—but after a recent visit, I knew I could definitely get down with the weather, the sea lions at La Jolla, the Gaslight District, Old Town, Santa Monica, the expansive beaches, and especially the slow foods, farm-to-fork movement, which seemed the antithesis of East Meadow's Grandma Slices and Rigatoni alla Vodka. In the dream scenario, I'd inspire my brother and sister to eventually follow me and open their respective yoga studio and hair salon there, too.

I stepped into a purple fuzzy robe and ran through the possibilities. If I sold the coffeehouse, or even kept it and refinanced my house, I could figure out a way to open a place in California—maybe a restaurant more in keeping with my current drive for less sugar and dairy. Or something else entirely, like renewing a false start in teaching, going back to magazine writing, or finally writing the book I knew I had in me. Newly inspired, I padded into my sponge-painted bedroom. Tossing my robe onto the wicker chair, I pulled on a ratty pair of sweatpants and the oldest, softest, most shredded T-shirt I could find and finagled myself between my cats to look up apartments for rent, but I found my eyes wandering up to the Gustav Klimt print I'd recently hung over my headboard.

I'd spotted the gilded print a few weeks earlier at a garage sale, wedged between a tricycle and fold-up table of mismatched china and silverware, and was entranced.

Obviously, I wasn't the first person in history to be captivated by *The Kiss*. This oil and gold leaf masterpiece of a man and a woman painted during the Austrian artist's "Golden Period," had been a subject of study since 1908. But there was something about it, beyond the artistry of the piece, beneath the warm, golden tones and the fluidity of the paint that called to me, made me drag it home, hang it over my bed, and ruin my seascape room.

Pang went the little alarm in my gut.

I ran my eyes over every detail of the couple in their intricate multicolored garb. His clothes contained black and white rectangles, hers, circles. And yet, taken together, their outfits—their beings—seemed to flow into one another and intertwine to the point where you didn't know where one began and the other ended.

Like the couple at the coffeehouse.

I could still see his face, unable to stop looking at her, and her face with that look of joy; it had been pure. However false I thought the concept of having it all with one person was, they believed it. And my friends, however briefly, had also believed. And my parents. And Shakespeare. And Klimt. And the Obamas…

It was possible that the "everything" narrative was so ingrained in us we couldn't help but believe it, even when it was false, and also possible that people were driven by their feelings to write the stories that insisted upon it, to paint circles and dots and swirls to prove it, to plan elaborate weddings to celebrate it.

What if it was me who was kidding myself?

I was happy alone. I loved being alone. But *if* such a person existed, what would it be like to meet him? What would it be like to feel, with absolute certainty, *whatever* it was that people felt?

I sat with this for a while, in that quiet alone space, wondering if my cynicism was simply a defense mechanism for the love narrative of my parents, which hadn't worked out, or if I'd somehow missed a connection.

I ran through the list: the poet who wanted me to be his sugar mama, the teacher who wanted me move to Alaska and bear him eight children, the tech guy who wanted me to wear a head scarf to meet his family, the restaurateur who wanted me to be his submissive, the construction worker who wanted me to accept his philandering, the Snapple route owner who wanted me to…I actually don't know what he wanted, and I don't think he did either. Still, I hadn't wanted anything with any of them.

I sat up and blew my nose. I also hadn't even allowed myself to entertain the concept of having an "everything." But now that I was warming up to the idea, now that I wanted to at least acknowledge the possibility that not every artist, writer, and friend, who insisted upon it, was delusional, what was I supposed to do about it?

Place your order with the Universe, I'd been advised in a "Tools for Change" class.

Should I? Nah, that was silliness. Then again, so was housing a $350, twenty-two volume Zohar in my bookcase for "protection" and tying expensive red yarn around my wrist to absorb "evil eye." And yet, so far, my house hadn't burned down, and I hadn't slipped on any banana peels.

I cracked my knuckles, turned on my laptop and opened a Word document, entitling it, *Dear Universe. Can you please send me my…* I snorted, hesitant to write the word. Did I even believe in the word? Was it possible that I had not a "star-crossed" lover but a *star-matched* lover in this sea of six to seven billion people, who I'd been split from at our…what was it the rabbi had said…at our spiritual birth? "…*soulmate,*" I wrote for the first time in my life.

I then sealed the document with imaginary hot wax and closed my laptop as metaphorical feathers swirled around me and the flame of the illusionary candle I'd lit went out.

Actually, nothing happened.

"I knew he was the one because when we were apart, I felt a piece of myself missing."

- L.F., Massapequa, married twelve years.

SIRE

A few months later, I smoothed my hair part with anti-frizz serum and dressed in skinny jeans, silver hoop earrings, high-heeled booties, and a blousy, off-the-shoulder burgundy sweater. My denim skirt matched better, but I didn't want to seem like I was trying too hard for an 11:00 a.m. Starbucks meet-and-greet. Also, I didn't want to try too hard.

My Dear Universe letter had proved a bust, and I'd once again set my sights on San Diego. As for the date I was about to go on, as sane as this guy had sounded, he was still an online match.

Soon after my Klimt meltdown, my friend Jay knocked on my door and insisted that I sign up to Match.com. Reluctant, but also noting the synchronicity of that door knock, I answered the profile questions with as much seriousness as I could summon.

What's your favorite food? The questionnaire asked, while Jay peered over my shoulder, blowing on her freshly painted blood red nails she would destroy the next day while scraping finger paint off her kindergarten desks.

"The first bite of Tofurky before you cave and admit you are eating rubber," I typed.

"You'll scare guys away," she said.

Who do you most admire? "The person who invented plastic shoelace tips," my fingers answered before my mind had time to process the stupidity of the question.

"Come on. I need to live vicariously through you," Jay said.

"Sorry, but if this phantom person doesn't have a sense of humor, I don't want to meet him. Besides, you should set up your profile."

"Not until I lose a hundred pounds."

"Then let me do it my way." I hit upload, sans a photo—six years shy of having a working camera phone, it was too much work.

The emails had pinged, and I'd scrolled though, amused and disgusted, but mostly disgusted. One man was angry that I hadn't posted a picture and tried to pick a fight over it, ending his rant with the accusation that I was an obese, ugly coward.

"Precisely the opposite," I'd begun to respond, developing an argument that I was very confident in my looks, and then back spaced. Truthfully, I was somewhat confident, in that I felt average-looking, really—five-foot-six-ish, one-hundred-thirty-five-ish pounds, brown eyes, brownish hair, skin that tanned dark in summer and turned freckled pale in winter—nothing that would win me a modeling contract with the Ford Agency. But I supposed I could pull it together with a strategic outfit and a blow-out. Could I stand to tone up a bit? Who couldn't? Sure, I had major insecurity about the red, dime-sized dots of psoriasis that mottled my elbows and knees and crawled along my torso like angry, inflamed misshapen beetles, a disorder inherited from my Dad and his Russian Jewish genes. Somehow, I had bypassed inheriting my mother's smooth Dutch skin, but I supposed everyone had something. Still, this jerk didn't need to know any of that. In fact, this jerk didn't need to know anything about me.

Delete, delete, delete. I'd shut my computer and walked away, only to return to the site a few months later to remove my profile, when I found a voice of sanity in the cuckoos' nest:

"Hi there. Something about your profile seems intriguing. Want to swap photos?"

Complete sentences? A direct request for a photograph with no insult attached? I perused his answers. Like me, this man seemed to be hiding behind humor, revealing only a piece of himself. I also noticed that he'd ignored my parameters of being within six years of my age, never married, and no kids. He was ten years older, divorced, and had a girl, nine, and a boy, fourteen. I could have interpreted this rebuff as arrogant, but for some reason I read it instead as confident. He seemed like a person who didn't feel the need to play by the rules.

A person, who, in his own way, lived outside the margins.

I sent him a photo, a full-length shot of me in San Diego, standing in front of the Kabbalah Center, a sign that was clearly legible and may as well have read "fair warning." He didn't flinch. Five minutes later he sent me a 4 x 6 shot of his face, which, other than showing me a set of symmetrical teeth, was hard to make out.

The teeth were nice, though.

Roasted coffee scented the air, steamers coughed and gurgled. People ordered *talls* and *grandes* with the same self-importance found during a Broadway show intermission. I reminded myself that a similar snobbery had afforded me a livelihood for almost a decade. I scanned the room, reluctantly admiring the retail section that looked impeccable and alluring—way better than my lone countertop display of Japanese teapots and infusers with handwritten signs, which still, mind-bogglingly, hadn't garnered one sale—and spotted him. He was impossible to miss. Head and shoulders above the crowd, he floated toward me.

"Heather?" I titled my face toward his air space, somewhere between the hanging signs directing the masses to "order" and "pick up."

"I'm Jon." His large hand absorbed mine in a firm grip: soft skin, white-collar—a hand that finalized deals in boardrooms, different from my own weathered hand, worn from dishwashing soap and espresso cleanser. "I have to say, you look even better in person."

He's a man, I thought, not a boy, not an adolescent, not a player, not a macho type. I realized in that instant I had never thought of any of the men I'd dated as *men*. Somehow, some way, they had registered in my mind as boys, guys, and dudes, which was strange considering how very attracted I was to the Harrison Fords, Denzel Washingtons, and John Hamms of the world.

"You do, too," I said. He had dark, c-shaped curls gelled tightly to his head and a mustache and goatee, a look classically reminiscent of a Greek Roman figure. His eyes, a woodsy-green and sparkling with intelligence, transported me to a log cabin in a remote forest where he would be wearing a lumberjack flannel shirt and jeans. Wait, what was that about? I didn't know, but it was a hot image, and I was there with him, feeling feminine, womanly, petite. The yin to his tall, six-foot-six, broad yang. What the hell was happening?

"Are you an athlete?" I asked. "Not that I follow sports, but you look...familiar."

"No, but a lot of people ask me that. Apparently I look like Carlos Chivara?"

"Who?"

"I think he's on *Desperate Housewives?*"

"I don't watch that."

"Me neither. But...*you* look really familiar, too."

"Alyssa Milano, I heard once? And when I was younger and tanner and had an affinity for headbands, I made it as a finalist in a Whitney Houston-look-a-like contest."

He laughed. "I guess I can see both...but..." He trailed off and shook his head, as if to say that my celebrity doppelgangers couldn't explain this odd sense of knowing me.

"Excuse me? Are you in line?" A woman pierced our bubble, and we motioned for her to go ahead.

"We should probably order something." He stepped into the roped area, and as he did, his hand grazed the small of my back. It barely touched my sweater, but I could feel its heat radiating, the way Reiki might feel—if I could bring myself to subscribe to the idea of being healed by invisible energy. For all my open-mindedness, I did occasionally draw the line.

We edged forward. I tried fixing my gaze on other things, but honestly, I couldn't take my eyes off him. It was like looking directly at the sun when you know you shouldn't, but you can't help it.

"So, tell me." He absorbed my face, as if I, too, were the most interesting creature in the world to him, and—here's the part I really liked—as if there was nothing wrong with locking his gaze on me. "Where have you been for the last seven years?"

"Well, that's a loaded question!"

He laughed, then waited for my answer. I had to at least *try* for nonchalance. "Living life. How about you?"

"Living life." He smiled, and I recognized beneath the smile, a look of disbelief. *How had he managed to do it without me?*

This was getting crazy. We approached the chalkboard of obnoxious, though smartly marketed, beverages.

"I'm thinking espresso," I said. "You?"

"Too much frill for me. Just coffee," he told the barista.

We took our drinks to a corner table.

"Now tell me everything there is to know about you," he said.

I loved that he didn't even try to conceal his enthusiasm. "You first."

He nodded, seeming to appreciate my strategy. He told me about his background in computer engineering and finance. He was smart and worldly, rattling off factual details about current world events, politics, and economic markets.

I knew less about these things, I admitted, mostly because I didn't like connecting to the negativity of the news. It bummed me out, not to mention how much I disliked having the electromagnetic energy of the television infiltrating my living room in the evening.

"I've never heard anyone talk like you," he said.

"What do you mean?"

"I mean, 'the third eye'? I never heard anyone talk about it...so casually. I don't think I even knew there was a third eye. Don't we just have two?" He motioned left and right of his nose.

"But life with only two eyes can get boring."

"You know what? It can." He leaned back. "Your turn."

I told him about the coffeehouse and about my desire to do more, about the ten-year cycle and San Diego.

"Well, you can't go there now!"

I reminded him that we'd known each other for an hour.

"But you can't!"

I laughed. He looked at me seriously. I had dated a stalker once, but this wasn't that. This was earnestness. The weird part? I suddenly knew there was no way I could go to San Diego either. But weren't we at least supposed to pretend?

"A bit presumptuous?" I tried.

"You know you can't," he said, not taking my playfulness seriously.

"Well, I'll admit...*this*...has definitely thrown a little monkey wrench into the mix."

He smiled his wide smile, and I felt...sunshine wash over me? This was nuts! And exhilarating.

More, more, more. He wanted to hear every detail about me. I told him about the movies I liked and the books I'd read. He had never heard of most of them, but he liked that my taste was "out of the box" as much as I liked that his taste was "in the box." He liked that I was a dreamer, and I liked that he was a skeptic. He liked that I was creative and worked with my hands, and I liked that he was intellectual and worked with his mind (he was running a hedge fund at the time).

"Now tell me about this Kabballah stuff," he said.

"Hmmm. Do I tell you about how I almost fell into a cult

first? Or how I now have what I think is a healthy relationship with it?"

"The cult."

So I told him about how seven years earlier I'd fallen too far off the grid. He was shocked at some of the things I shared, such as how when I'd first taken courses, I'd connected with an institution that was shameless about taking donations, and I'd not only donated a lot of money but had become seriously brainwashed into believing that if I didn't attend their events, I would be cursed; and how not "tithing" ten percent of my income would—how to put it—destroy my soul.

"That's really hard to imagine," he said. "You seem way too smart for something like that. That seems like something a more clueless person would do."

Well, two things about that.

One—I had been that clueless person once, the kind who had made those kinds of choices, choices probably traced back to childhood, before I'd learned to come up for air, and before I'd developed a sense of humor about some of my self-improvement adventures. (I'd needed to go deep to deal with my mother's abandonment, my father's subsequent shut down, and my six-year stint in foster care, to name a few of the greatest hits.)

Two—even though I'd finally woken up and disconnected from that crazy cult through the help of literature, art, time, and age, the fibers from my childhood remained, the way threads of invisible fiberglass insidiously enter the lungs and lay low until many years later, when they create breathing complications. But even I didn't know that at the time.

So I simply said, "I was young and stupid."

His background was much more grounded and linear. He had an unremarkable childhood and had never joined a cult. He'd worked at IBM out of college as a chip designer. After a few years of that, he'd felt pigeonholed in the nine to five world and when he saw his friends making money as stockbrokers, he took the "Series 7." I liked his straight-forward way of telling stories. He honed in on a point and nailed it to the wall. He liked my airy, circling storytelling, how I interrupted myself to interrupt myself, weaving four tales in one, and then, as he said, "miraculously brought it all home."

Before we knew it three hours had passed.

"We *had* to have met before," he said. "Here comes that déjà vu feeling again."

I'd been having it, too, only my vision had moved on from the lumberjack scene to Mexico, circa 1500. At some point during our chat an image flashed before me of Jon in a different incarnation, dressed as a general on horseback, extending his hand, hoisting me onto the back of his horse. He not only seemed familiar, but familial. Was it our Jewish background? Mine consisting of mysticism courses; his consisting of traditional Judaism, punctuated by Hebrew school and a bar mitzvah. Or was it simply that we'd grown up in the Northeast and shared a suburban culture? Maybe it was that we were both one of three children, although I was the attention-seeking middle child and he was the pioneering older one. Or that we somewhat looked alike? He was Lithuanian, Polish, and English, but our eye shape, noses, smiles, and long limbs, were all similar. An evolutionist might describe us as the right "phenotype" for each other.

It's something else, I thought as I excused myself to the bathroom. He stood for me and made room for me to pass, tilting his head as I did. And then I had it.

He *literally* resembled the male figure in the Klimt print. Though only the back of the man's head was visible in the painting, Jon had the same lilt, the same curly hair, the same circles, dots, and swirls reaching for me.

"Everything okay?"

"Everything's great," I said, slightly breathless, and went to splash cold water on my cheeks.

21

"We should probably give up this table at some point," he said when I returned. "Not that I want to leave. I could stay here all day. Tell me that I can see you this weekend."

Seeing as we spent previous lifetimes together, I felt like saying, *I don't see why not.* But if thinking it sounded outrageous, saying it seemed nuts. I needed to regroup.

I tried to ground myself, walking on the concrete sidewalk arm in arm with him that Friday night, as we dipped inside a Belgian restaurant in Rockville Center, but I found myself floating anyway. The place was small, dark, and chic—so dark, the hostess had to use a small flashlight to walk us to our table.

Was I imagining things, I wondered, that people were giving way for us? I wasn't, I decided, though it had nothing to do with me and everything to do with him. He gave off a sense of authority that made people ask him how long the wait was or what time the music was starting. At one point, before we were seated, a man picked up a piece of paper from the floor and tapped Jon's shoulder. "Sir, is this yours?" The way the man deferred, I thought for a split second he'd called him "sire."

"Good?" Jon asked as we settled into our hard-backed seats.

"It's great."

"I've got your number."

I smiled, even though I was sweating and had been since Starbucks. Regrouping had only made things worse, as I'd run through our meeting with disbelief, adrenaline, and insecurity. I *knew* something all right—I had left planet Earth and nothing seemed real, including this man who seemed literally perfect. Tall, handsome, smart, articulate, Ivy League through and through. I was City University with a broken upbringing and skin that could rival an iguana's. Seriously, did he have even *one* flaw?

"The reviews are excellent. But if it's not...hip enough... we can go somewhere else." He looked concerned, and I felt a dash of mojo return.

"It's perfect," I said, observing his cream-colored boat neck sweater with fresh eyes. Not something I'd seen in recent catalogues or stores.

He sensed me watching and looked up from his menu. "What are you thinking of getting?"

"Hmmm, *maybe* the organic, free-range chicken," I hedged. After a ten-year stint as a vegetarian, I still felt guilty about reincorporating some animal products to help calibrate my skin issues.

"Do they have that here?" He scoured the menu and found it. "Interesting. Let me ask you—I mean, *really*. Is there any real difference between organic and regular chicken?"

"Without a doubt," I said, knowing that what I wanted to say next wasn't exactly going to come across as romantic-speak, but honestly, he'd asked. And, if whatever was happening was *real*, then I needed to be myself. And that self would never turn down an opportunity to preach about the horrors of conventional factory farming.

I skimmed though the basics: the insanity of growth hormones; cramming animals into cages; depriving them of normal functions, like being able to peck (they burn their beaks off) or even just move; the ineffective and dangerous practice of jacking them up with antibiotics, when—surprise, surprise—they got sick from the crowded conditions...

"Wow, that's really horrible." He put his menu down. "Soooo...I'm guessing I'm going to offend the shit out of you when I order the osso bucco?"

I half spit out some water. Apparently, he'd also decided he wasn't going to be anything other than his own true self—especially if it meant deprivation of any kind. He was into food, I could tell, and not just by how he'd been devouring the bread basket and asking for more of those "cinnamon rolls with the raisins and some extra butter," but by how he began to eye my plate halfway through our meal.

"Help yourself." I pushed it toward him.

"Only if you're not going to eat it." He chewed with the thoughtfulness of a food critic. "Interesting."

"What?"

"Tastes just like chicken."

I laughed. This was new, having someone hold up a mirror to my beliefs and make me laugh about them. My exes, I realized then, had pretty much always accepted what I'd said as gospel.

After he'd eaten his dinner and half of mine, he leaned back and looked at the dessert menu. I noticed a little extra flesh along his waistline, which I hadn't noticed before, a cute pinch-an-inch. It was a minor imperfection, but I took it.

"Chocolate mousse," he told the waitress.

I didn't have a major stake in dessert, but I could tell he was hoping for some of mine.

"Lemon sorbet?" I suggested, then saw his scowl. "Apple crumble?" I tried again.

We drove back to my place, and I couldn't help feeling as if I was watching the world go by like it was a movie set. On the way, I grilled him on life before that moment, the person he was ten times over before being a forty-four-year-old divorced father of two on a date with me, beginning with his boy self in southern New Jersey. I learned of the eight-year-old boy who idolized his father, a veterinarian and professor at the University of Pennsylvania, who'd written a book, *The Endocrinology System of Dogs*, before anyone knew dogs had endocrine systems. I learned of the sixteen-year-old who'd just lost his father and took a job at a deli so he could bring home money to his mother, who was struggling to pay the mortgage, medical school bills, and raise three kids on her nurse's salary. Barson's Deli. His claim to fame was making coleslaw, immersing his forearms into vats of cabbage, mayo, and vinegar. Also, slicing paper thin turkey breast for picky customers, once slicing the pad off his finger.

He wiped his feet on my entrance mat and stepped into my living room, scanning its rustic-farmhouse-meets-modern-vintage look: velvet-tufted cushions on the retro rocking chair; rust-colored velour panels flanking the windows; vanilla scented candles in glass lanterns; creamy yellow walls; wrought-iron owl on the mantel of the wood-burning fireplace; sleek, taupe couch with chenille pillows; various pieces from the Pottery Barn catalogue. There among the décor, and in some of the framed photos he studied, were clues to some of the earliest people I'd been, too. The six-year-old, who hoped her parents would come for her. The fourteen-year-old, who'd worked at a luncheonette and dreamed of a way out of her life. The twenty-one-year-old, who rode on the back of a bad boy's motorcycle, thinking they might crash and deciding it would be okay to live fast and die young; the twenty-five-year-old, who decided she'd rather live, celebrate, and create.

"It feels so cozy," he said. "Like…a home."

I wanted to hug him. And buy him a cool new sweater. And nurture him. *What was that about?* He had a house, but my intuition told me it was a place where he could shower and sleep and hold Taco Tuesdays and sleepovers every other weekend, not a home.

I suppose people had always reminded me of animals. I'd always seen myself as a sort of deer in the woods, happy to roam the forest alone and find some leafy greens to munch on. In that moment, Jon, though he was built like a silverback gorilla, had the character of a lion, an animal who not only benefitted from having a lifelong mate beside him but who was built to travel with his pride. And this poor creature had been wandering the plains alone for the last seven years?

"Tell me about your dating life." I moved about the kitchen to make peppermint tea.

"You really don't want to hear about that."

I pulled it out of him. After his divorce, he'd dated a flight attendant, a lawyer, a veterinarian assistant, and a teacher. The veterinarian assistant lasted for two nights. She'd showed up at his house wearing only a fur coat; she'd left him notes in his underwear drawer, which spooked him. The teacher had lasted five years. She had been great, but it just wasn't right. There had never been "the one," not even in his marriage.

I saw him then as his college self, the lanky twenty-two-year-old with black curly hair, friends with a girl who he would ask to move in with him during senior year. "When we graduated, it seemed like the next step was to get married, I guess. Like you, I didn't have much guidance."

"Did you ever...grow to be in love?"

"Grow? I don't know. I mean, I loved her. But different than...." He picked up an incense holder and smelled it. "Like I said, we were best friends. It's strange to say because we were married, but we were never really romantic."

I nodded. "You were missing the other triangle tips."

"Wait, what's this about?"

"I'll tell you another time. Keep going."

"Actually, let's talk about something else." He came up behind me and draped his arms around me as I poured tea into ceramic mugs. It felt amazing to be folded in his arms, but his hand was dangerously close to the bottom of my shirt, where bare, rough skin lay within touch. I squirmed out of his hold.

"It's my turn to hear everything." I held out a hot mug.

He had no choice but to take it, following me to the living room couch. I dragged more out of him, more people he had been: a young father living in East Fishkill, when he worked for IBM; the suited Manhattanite who woke at 5:30 a.m. to trade stocks, then came come home at 7:00 p.m. to lift weights in the basement. "Ten years paased. We were busy. We had Eddie and Emily. And eventually, she resented me."

"Why?"

He shrugged. "I don't know. Probably because she hadn't really solidified a career before the kids. Then staying home. I guess at some point, she felt lost. I guess it happens. She hated me at the end, though. It was rough."

It sounded difficult to naïve, single me and impossible to identify with. No matter how many times I'd heard the same story of a woman losing herself in a marriage, the "how" and "why" it could happen in modern, feminist times still confused me.

He set his mug down and inched closer, tucked a strand of hair behind my ear. "But I'll be honest. I never felt anything like this…"

"Jon—"

He leaned in. "You know I'm going to have to kiss you now."

"There's—"

His lips landed on mine, strong. I kissed back. He slid one hand behind my lower back, pulled me closer, dropped the other to my waist, closer still, as his hand followed the guitar curve down my hip and back up, along my rib. I tugged at my shirt, to keep it down as a barrier to conceal the roughness of my skin, but I couldn't stay on the ground. I began to float, somewhere above us. He was with me, past the ceiling, into sky. I remembered a book I'd read as a teenager—one of the books my mother had left behind—about people travelling to the astral plane when they were sleeping. It was called *The Highlands of Heaven* and described how when people drifted to sleep, their souls would lift out of their bodies, connected only by some kind of umbilical cord plugged into their solar plexuses. What bullshit! I'd thought. And yet here we were, *awake* and hovering, tethered to each other's kiss below. I willed myself back, tugged down my shirt.

"I know," he whispered. He meant he knew we weren't going to have sex.

"That's not it. I mean it is, but…you don't know everything."

"I know everything I need to know."

"Please. Let me show you." I pulled up my sleeve to reveal my elbow, then looked away, not wanting to see his disappointment.

"What am I looking at?"

"My emotional war wounds," I said. "My ultimate shame."

"Yeah, but what is it? Eczema?"

"Psoriasis."

"Heather, you've got to be kidding me! Get over here. You know this doesn't take away from your beauty one bit. Are you telling me anyone's ever cared about this?"

They hadn't; I had never cared until now.

"Well, if it makes you feel any better, I have Keratoconus." He explained about the degenerative distortion of his corneas, a disease he'd been dealing with since he was thirty, which made simple tasks like driving, watching TV, or reading a book difficult. He wore a double set of contact lenses, piggyback it was called, hard lenses over soft lenses. His greatest fear was blindness.

"Okay, now I feel like an asshole," I said.

"Don't." He laughed. "Though I would take your skin over my eyes any day of the week."

At two a.m., we reluctantly pried ourselves away, with plans for lunch the following day.

I collapsed on my bed, under the Klimt print, exhausted and wired.

"Holy Moly," I said aloud, to whomever and whatever was listening—to the sky, to the air and clouds, to the stars and moon, to gods and mystics, to Gustav, and maybe some old white-haired female sage made of vapor and pixie dust who lived on Vega.

I'd be damned if that Universe didn't know what she was doing.

"It's not enough to love your partner; you have to adore them."

- *D.F., Baldwin, married forty-three years*

COURTSHIP

Would I have drunk the Kool-Aid right then and there?

Damn straight.

You know that montage scene in movies where the in-love couple walks hand in hand on the beach, shares a tub of popcorn at the movies, and downs a milkshake using two straws? That was us—substituting a soy, Spirulina shake for dairy, and reducing the number of straws to one; he was a good sport, but he wasn't a fan of Spirulina's grainy texture.

"And this is from a *pond?*" Jon asked.

"It's a high-protein algae with all the essential amino acids."

"So it's pond scum."

I laughed. I had never thought of it that way. "Basically, yes."

"I think I'll enjoy watching you enjoy it." He sat back in my kitchen chair, amused, but also truly enjoying watching me drink a protein shake.

I began to believe in the narratives, in all the impassioned literature, and in my friends' initial stories. With each passing day, I believed in their magic and power and rethought my lampshade quote. Love was not something we made up to make more of our biological selves. It *was*, in part, biological. It was primal and basic and tangible and earthly and, at the same time, heady. Although it would be some time before I read about Helen Fischer's concept of the "love drive" and the "addiction of love" inside the brain, I could practically feel the dopamine spiking.

We were like teenagers. For the next week and a half, we separated only to work—unable to imagine life before meeting—and even then he visited me, occupying a corner armchair to work on his computer, keeping one eye on me as I rang up lattes and schmoozed with the tatted, pierced twenty-something regulars who planned to change the world.

Afterward, we would go next door to the Wantagh Inn, an Irish cop bar, and listen to a cover band, or to the corner diner where he would order his fries "hot and extra, extra crispy," and then poach some of my "cold, soggy ones." We drove to Long Beach, parked down a side street, and made our way past the singles' bars I used to frequent—the floors sticky with beer, the bathrooms smelling faintly of vomit—back in what felt like a lifetime ago. We climbed onto the icy boardwalk that stretched for miles to watch the wide expanse of the Atlantic Ocean crash and roll before us, to watch the world unfurl together.

I could feel myself morphing—this thirty-four-year-old person with her hard edges. She was softening, opening her eyes to new points of view, and wondering—and hoping—that she wasn't delusional about this inexplicable connection.

We still hadn't consummated the deal—trying, as I think we both had secretly decided, to allow a respectable amount of time to pass. But at the end of the second week, as I was blow-drying my hair, getting ready to drive to his place for the first time, he made his intentions clear.

"There's a snowstorm coming," he texted. "So pack an overnight bag."

My stomach danced, even as I worried—what if sex wasn't perfect? What if we had only two points of the triangle?

"Should I bring my footie pajamas?"

"No pajamas. Just a toothbrush."

Nervous, in a good kind of way, I made my way north, following Route 107, past the Walmart and Kmart shopping centers of Levittown and the delicious curry houses of Hicksville, and then through Bethpage, home to Grumman, whose toxic plume, already spreading and contaminating local water wells, had yet to be discovered. I could have been looking at the seascape of La Jolla, but I knew that longer mattered. Meeting him had cast the dull landscape of Long Island in Technicolor.

The snow had started to fall in chunks, and I succumbed to the slow crawl of cars. Jon texted nonstop, admonishing me to drive carefully and to stop reading his texts.

I shot back at a red light. "Then stop texting!" Meanwhile, I hoped he'd never stop texting, never stop caring. No one had ever doted over my every waking second like this—not in adulthood, and definitely not in childhood.

Love, I decided right then and there, as much as it was about how we felt about another, was equally about the way that other made us feel about ourselves.

"Smart? Beautiful? Kind? Funny? Sexy? I can't believe no one has scooped you up yet," he'd said, just a week or so earlier. Feeling smart, beautiful, kind, funny, and sexy, I'd returned the favor. "Smart, handsome, sexy, a giant teddy bear? Not to mention, a LEO, of all signs."

Jon tried to understand the "voodoo" and "magic" of astrology I talked about. But to him, stars had always been burning masses of gas, not roadmaps to our personalities. Little did he know that his comebacks made me secretly wonder if I'd been silly, blindly believing in "sometimes encouraging fiction, sometimes discouraging fiction," as he put it.

In just a short amount of time, I'd begun to see our connection not only as a classic case of opposites attracting, but also as our own version of two characters in Shel Silverstein's *The Missing Piece Meets the Big O*, in which two distinctly different pieces, one a triangle and one a circle with a triangle cutout, click together to complete each other.

"What's that?" he'd asked when he'd seen the ionizing water filter piped into my kitchen sink.

"Oh, that's an alkaline system. It separates water molecules and alkalizes the water."

"So, in other words, it's complete bullshit?"

"You don't believe in it?"

He'd gotten a good chuckle out of that one. "It's not a matter of believing, Heather. It's a matter of chemistry. Water is already neutral on the pH scale. It has an equal number of H+ and OH- ions. That makes it neutral. Not alkaline or acidic."

He'd studied engineering in college. He was a person of facts and figures, weights and measures, charts and graphs. I was a person of imagery and inklings. He looked for the holes in a scientific theory (or, in this case, holes in a pseudo-scientific theory); I looked for the story in it.

Meanwhile, he had never been more entertained by a person's quirkiness, by my love of stories, art, theatre, and music. That's because scientists and artists need each other, as one of my old-time favorite movies, *Contact*, suggested when scientist Jodie Foster visited another planet and tried to describe it in her recorder. "They should have sent a poet... beautiful, beautiful..."

"Want a glass of bullshit anyway?" I'd offered.

"Please," he'd said, licking his dry lips.

The snow fell in cotton balls, and I moseyed along, making my way toward him. Soon, the congestion of the scenery opened. The north shore was a whole different world from the south shore of Long Island, less dense, fewer shopping centers, more land per house, chock full of tall trees. They were old growth, mature trees with thick trunks and wide canopies that caught the snow and turned the scene fairy tale-esque, making me wonder why people on the south shore—like my next-door neighbors—were so intent on getting rid of theirs.

I remembered a weekend customer, a grandmother from Merrick, telling me how she'd cut down the tree closest to her bedroom window because the branches scratched annoyingly at her siding, and about the utter regret she'd felt realizing she no longer had birds to wake her, or leaves to shield her from her neighbor's windows. I'd listened, feigning sympathy. Meanwhile, that poor tree! How did she think *it* felt?

I forked left toward Oyster Bay, a nautical hamlet that abutted the Long Island Sound. If Long Island is an alligator head—which it looks like from a bird's eye view—with the neck touching Manhattan and the bottom jaw housing Montauk and the Hamptons, Oyster Bay sat on the Alligator's head (while East Meadow was swallowed in its throat). Antique shops and restaurants filled up the storefronts. Christmas lights illuminated the snow beneath them. I turned right at the end of Main Street and followed Jon's directions until I reached a residential area, and then, a private development with a winding, twisting drive. It was pretty but also somehow reminiscent of the *Poltergeist* neighborhood with identical homes cut from the same model—gray cedar shake shingles, mullioned windows, and what appeared to be a communal backyard as large and lush as a golf course, which the houses horseshoed around.

"Why Oyster Bay?" I'd asked, during one of our beach outings, and he'd explained the town was close to his kids' house (and NYC, parkways, and airports) but was still remote enough to enjoy the country feel of the north shore. But mainly because he loved being near the water.

"The south shore has some great places by the water, too," I'd said.

"I can't do the south shore."

"Yeah, I guess it's far from your kids."

"No, I just could never live there. Everyone clustered together like that, living on top of each other."

"You *do realize* that you're completely insulting me since I own a house there?"

"Yeah, but, come on. You didn't really know what you were buying."

It was true. I had "thrown a dart" at my house, choosing a box in a town within a five-mile radius of work. I had done the same when purchasing most of the major items in my life, like the Jeep Wrangler before my Jetta. I drove it off the lot without so much as a test-drive, a major regret I'd have to live with for two years until, mercifully, my "mail truck" was stolen. But I didn't consider myself above my neighborhood, so much as I felt disconnected to its family-centric lifestyle, although, arguably, that was a superiority complex of another kind.

He'd chosen carefully, I saw, as I pulled into the long, winding cul-de-sac. His house sat in the center of the horseshoe curve, with the best view of the sprawling, fertilized back yard. He waved from the open bank of the two-door garage, wearing jeans and moccasin style slippers, and signaled me forward, gestured for me to stop, turn the wheel, come this much more forward, no, stop, okay, go. It was kind of funny. I mean, I *was* a grown woman and knew how to pull into a garage, but it was also beyond adorable.

"You made it." He escorted me out of the driver's seat. "Where's your bag?"

"I didn't bring it."

"Pop the trunk." Meaning, you and I both know you're sleeping over.

I opened the trunk, and he strapped my duffle bag over his shoulder, tucked my arm into the crook of his, and walked us toward the inner garage door that led inside the house.

"I was getting worried. It's really starting to come down out there," he said. We turned to see the snow falling in large pieces. "But now you're safe," he said, hitting the fat button on the wall. The garage door closed on the white scenery outside and my life before meeting him.

"I got some Chinese food—no MSG." He wiped his slippers on the mat. "I didn't even know places still used that."

"Most don't, but you never know. Thanks for asking."
I took off my boots, not loving being flatfooted next to
him—it put extra strain on my neck to see his face—but I
didn't want to walk through his place with my shoes on. It
was impressive—and fancy—not a term I used often, but
one that seemed fitting to describe the high-end feel of this
four-thousand square foot center hall colonial with its fifteen
foot ceilings, polished oak floors, open floor plan, and what
looked like real artwork hanging on the walls (not some sec-
ond-hand garage sale Klimt).

"Come. I'll give you the tour first," he said.

As we walked through the living room, I asked him about
the art, and he pointed out a few pieces by Fazzino, a pop-up
artist I'd never heard of, as well as lesser, more obscure pieces
by an artist named Posillico. There was a wooden sculpture,
six feet high, of a twisted tribal female figure and a solid
sterling silver elephant the size of small dog, which sat on a
marble pedestal.

"Those better not be real tusks," I said.

"They're not. At least I don't think so." He examined them.
I did too. Neither of us could tell.

"Where did you get it? And *why?*"

"New Orleans." He shrugged. "It seemed cool at the time."

There were more treasures from past travels. In the kitchen:
Steuben glass sculptures. Down the hallways: gilded frames
around even the simplest prints. In the living room: tufted,
fine silk chairs. Upstairs, the kids' bedrooms were magazine
perfect, almost unlived in. Emily's was a purple Victorian
paradise with a dark green wrought-iron canopy bed with
lavender and white chiffon panels framed around a bedding
design of purple roses and green ivy. The dressers were antique, ivory-colored, hand-painted. Eddie's held dark wooden
furniture and masculine bedding in browns, navy, and cream.
In the Jack and Jill bathroom, show towels and decorative
soaps abounded. This was his *divorce* bachelor pad? And yet,

I had been quasi-right in my guess that his house was not a home. It was a museum.

But it was the item in the den that stopped me in my tracks. "You've got to be kidding me," I said. "You have a *throne?*"

"It's not a throne, Heather." He was amused. "It's a chair."

A chair that would dwarf the average-sized human. The back rose six feet from the ground and was made of elaborately carved wood and brown tufted leather. The arms, also wooden, held matching leather elbow rests and two carvings of lion heads on their hand rests. The feet were chiseled to resemble two paws.

"See." He sat down to make his point.

"Now all you need is a crown and one of those oversized turkey legs from Disneyland."

"That's a bit of overkill, don't you think?"

But was it? It was amazing to me that he couldn't see what I was seeing.

We continued the tour downstairs, to the entertainment room in the walk-out basement with state-of-the-art equipment, which he was actually more proud of than anything else in the house. He jacked up the music and swapped out special effects to show me its full capabilities. It was kind of geeky. And, of course, adorable.

Last stop was back upstairs in the master bedroom with a California king-size bed on a par with the throne. Its headboard was eight feet high and constructed of solid mahogany, and the brown, gold, and burgundy paisley-bedding looked straight out of a Ralph Lauren commercial.

"I had a decorator at my old place, which you would have hated." His first bachelor pad, he told me, had been the Ferguson castle. Located a few towns from Oyster Bay, in Huntington, overlooking the Long Island Sound, it had been deemed an historical property and had often been featured in architectural magazines. Well, that explained not only the bedding, but other furnishings I hadn't said a word about such as the navy blue satin-upholstered armchairs with gold piping and the banquet-sized dining room table with custom-designed linens and tablecloths, all of which made for an interesting contrast against traditional white moldings.

"Well, your house is beautiful," I said.

He shifted his feet on the carpet, looking uncomfortable. We were standing four feet from the bed and it suddenly occurred to me that maybe he wasn't as smooth as he'd been presenting himself. Perhaps he was as geeky with intimacy as he was with engineering and electronics.

Thank god. I was still nervous as hell. Forget perfection. What if it…totally *sucked?*

"How about something to drink?" he asked.

"Do you have straight vodka?"

"I hope so." We went back to the safety of the living room and nestled into the couch, iced drinks in hand. Something was on his mind. "I appreciate that you like this place, but it's just not where I want to be right now."

"You don't like Oyster Bay?"

It wasn't Oyster Bay, he explained, it was his status in life. He'd sold the Ferguson castle after 9/11; most of his money had been in the stock market, and he'd had to downsize to start over. This house was all he had left. The hedge fund he'd recently started, as well as some other entrepreneurial financial endeavors, weren't panning out the way he'd hoped, and he hesitated to tell me he was in between earnings at the moment.

"Can I just tell you something?" I said. "And I totally mean this. I LOVE that you have no job right now."

"What? Why?"

Because we can start over together the way young people do.

"I just do." I put my arms around his neck. "Want me to take care of you? I would love to take care of you."

"Yeah? And how would you do that?"

"How about I open a string of coffeehouses?"

"And what would I do?"

"Stay at home in your bathrobe." I shrugged. "Hell, become an alcoholic if you want."

"Hey!"

"Okay, fine, you can be the CEO."

"I can't do that."

"Why not? It's just coffee. People make such a big deal about coffee beans."

"Because any schlepp can be a CEO of something like that."

"Oh, my god!" I cracked up laughing. "You *do* realize that is not only the most egotistical thing you could say but a total dig to me?"

"Come on. You know what I mean. I need to feel good about what *I'm* doing."

"You're digging a bigger hole."

"I am, aren't I?" He kissed me. And kissed me again. "You know I think you're a rock star. But I have to be my own rock star, too. I'll figure it out." He tucked my hair behind my ear. "Should we go eat?" he asked.

"I'm starving," I said. He stood, tucked his arms beneath me, and scooped me off the couch. "You're not literally going to carry me across the threshold, are you?"

"I believe I am."

Outer space, the astral plane, wormholes, and far-off galaxies. As the last tip sharpened to a point, it was the moment when the angels smiled and threw a disco party.

Also, the sex was great. I gave it an eight out of ten. Minus two points for some awkward fumbling. But he was definitely a lion, which, if I was a deer, made us a perfect predator-prey match in nature.

Funny, it strikes me now, how back then I thought it a positive thing that predators absorb their prey.

"R-E-S-P-E-C-T."
 - *Beth Fox, Plainview, married forty years*

Court

The next morning, he made delicious, cheesy scrambled eggs, which was the best breakfast I'd had in a long time.

"They're just eggs," he said. But that's what I liked—their simplicity. When I made eggs, I over-complicated things by pan-frying zucchini and onion frittatas or baking roasted veggie quiches and usually ended up scraping the nauseating batch into the garbage.

He poured me a glass of orange juice and sat down. "So, I have my kids tonight. Are you cool with meeting them? I thought I'd bring them to the coffeehouse."

"Of course," I fibbed, inadequacy bubbling up. The one time a friend had asked me to babysit her two-year-old daughter, she'd returned home to find me mummified in blankets. "Oh, Heather," she'd sighed, knowing I had done anything and everything to keep her kid happy. How women dealt with children gracefully had always been one of life's great mysteries to motherless me. But I was now older and wiser, and, as I scraped the last bite of cheese from my plate, I told myself I'd been drawn to a man with children for a reason. "There is an opportunity in discomfort," the rabbi had once said. "A chance to learn and grow."

Of course, it also entered my mind that Jon had it pretty easy compared to me. While I had two complex beings to win over, he already had the affections of my cats who required mere indifference to purr.

"Unless you'd rather meet them on your day off. We can go bowling or something."

Did people still bowl? Wow. I'd been out of the mainstream loop for some time. But I wanted to reach for that opportunity.

"Tonight's good. Come whenever."

Dear Universe,
Please, oh please, let them like me.
Love, Heather

Jon beamed like a proud papa as he walked with his kids through the red velvet drapes framing the front door of The Cup.Eddie, almost as tall as his dad and full of fourteen-year-old gawkiness, ducked from habit under the exit sign, although there was no need; he could clear it by a good inch. He had a round face and curly black hair—much more of it than Jon. It was poofed and teased into a bulbous afro. On his navy hooded sweatshirt read the word STAFF in big yellow letters.

Emily shuffled in next to her brother. Tall for a nine-year-old, she wore pink and purple clothes and scanned the room with her large doe eyes framed within a curtain of blonde, shoulder-length hair.

"Hi, guys," I said—too loudly, I saw by their wide eyes—but I could barely hear myself. The place was in full swing, every table occupied. Music blared from the floor speakers as the performer sang about "Tommy's Mommy…she used to wear a swami…." We bumbled as we shook hands and ended up half hugging instead.

"Should we go in the back room to talk?" They shrugged, and I motioned for them to follow.

The back room was the room coveted by our customers. At eight by nine feet, it barely fit the gold velour couch, two crushed-velvet armchairs, and the antique coffee table be-tween them. As soon as we entered its vacuum, I realized my mistake. They liked it better where the action was. In there, I was Dad's new girlfriend.

"It's so great to finally meet you…" I searched for words. Man, was it quiet in there. "Your dad's told me so much about you guys."

"Cool," Eddie said. Emily shifted and half-smiled.

"Are you a bouncer?" I asked Eddie, nodding to his shirt.

"Nah. I just like wearing it."

"It's his handle," Jon said.

"Yeah, my teacher called me 'Staff Fro' one day, and the name kind of stuck."

"That's so funny!"

They shrugged, toe shifted, floor stared. "How about a snack?" Jon said. "You guys want something to eat?"

Of course. Why didn't I think of that? I thrust menus into their hands.

Eddie chuckled and read out loud: "Frozen Hot Chocolate: made with our top-secret marshmallow formula. What's the formula?"

"A teaspoon of Fluff," I said, divulging what most of our customers knew; it was one of the most frequently asked questions.

"That's the whole thing?"

"Yep."

He liked that, thank god.

"I can't decide between the Spicy Fries or the Smushed Blueberry Pie in a Mug," Emily said.

"Get both," I offered. She blinked her big eyes, as if to say *really?* I called the waitress over, seizing the opportunity to buy their happiness. French fries. Pie. Frozen Lemonade. Cake. Ice cream. I wasn't above bribery.

"Do you guys want to eat in here, or out there?"

"Out there," they chorused.

I spotted a table near the stage—thankfully the musician had taken a break. As we made our way over, I noticed Emily smoothing over her hair and Eddie tugging down his shirt, and the light bulb went off. They wanted me to like them too.

My heart bloomed. "So, Eddie, your dad tells me you're going to the Rockefeller Institute of Science this summer. Tell me about it."

"Yeah, I got a scholarship. It's pretty cool, as cool as these nerdy things go." He told me all about the program.

"Emily, you've been playing cello since you were five? Is it true your orchestra played at Carnegie Hall? I would love to see that one day."

"Thanks. Yeah, I'm pretty psyched about it. I love cello."

Even with all my lack of experience, as they talked, I could see these were no ordinary kids. They were intellectuals. "Indoor kids" was the term that came to mind and maybe even prodigies. They were both in the gifted and talented programs at their schools, and Eddie was also in the International Baccalaureate Program. The food came and they dug in, giving me a big thumbs-up.

"I'm so glad you like it. I've been battling with my soul to try and make things a little healthier here."

"I wouldn't," Eddie said.

"It's a coffeehouse," Emily said. "It's meant to be unhealthy."

"You mean you wouldn't want a vegan brownie sundae with coconut ice cream?" *Blah!* their faces said.

"By the way, Dad said you were an English major," Eddie said, sucking whipped cream out of a straw. "Did you ever read *To Kill a Mockingbird?*"

"Sure."

"What's it about?" He smiled pure charm. "I have an essay test on it tomorrow."

"He never reads the books," Emily said.

"Your dad told me you get all A-pluses."

He shrugged. "You just have to pay attention in class. It's pretty obvious what they want to read in the essay."

"Wow," I laughed. "That must be nice."

"I have to study." Emily fake-pouted.

"Well, if it makes you feel any better, so did I."

"I didn't," Jon said, smugly.

"You're just so awesome!" Eddie threw himself at Jon and smothered his father in kisses.

"Hey! Get off!" Jon tried to poke at Eddie's underarm and tickle him. Jon won and then started eating Eddie's leftover pie.

"God, Dad, why don't you eat the mug too?" Emily said.

I liked their dynamic, especially their collective goal to try and knock their dad down a notch.

"Seriously, who let this guy in here?" Eddie said. "Dad, you're too old for this place."

"I know the owner," Jon said.

"Well, he looks younger than he is," I said. It was true. I had more crow's feet than him.

"Yeah, but he looks as uncool as he really is," Eddie said.

"I'm cool," Jon said. "I'm *very cool.*" They shot him unconvinced looks. "Did I ever tell you that I drove across country my senior year in college?"

"Please not this story again," Eddie said, while Emily groaned.

Jon ignored them and recounted the time he'd driven across country, so he could intern at a California water company with a German student, who spoke no English but had responded to Jon's flyer in the Student Union. Their common language had been pot and Pink Floyd's *The Wall.*

"Loser," Eddie coughed into his hand.

"Sorry, Dad. No offense, but I don't know if I'd call that 'very cool,'" Emily said.

"Well, he's cool to me," I said, knowing with certainty, at last, that he wasn't. But he was my geeky, handsome engineer who could do complex math in his head and answer every question correctly in Strunk and White's *The Elements of Style* (I'd tested him). He was my working-on-becoming-a-ten lover who cooked delicious eggs, and was also, I was starting to see, a great dad.

They looked at me, puzzled. Maybe I wasn't as cool as I'd first seemed.

I suddenly wasn't—and I kind of liked it.

Over the next few weeks, I edged out from the margins and joined Jon at Emily's basketball games and dance recitals, finding myself touched by the commitment of parents on the sidelines and maybe even in admiration of those people I'd once accused of being boring. Seriously, was there anything more intense than seeing the nine-year-old you came to root for snag the ball and head down the court for a layup shot?

We made popcorn for movie night every other weekend, making our way through family films that not only gutted my heart but Jon's too. To see him bawling by the end of *Mrs. Doubtfire*, or, although he denied it, *Finding Nemo*, was the best part.

On Wednesdays, they invited me to eat dinner at their usual family spot, Uncle Dai's, one of many restaurants I'd never known existed before Jon, a local dive that served boxed wine, under-carbonated soda, and suspicious "chicken." Prey to the urban myth that the owners trapped and killed pigeons out back, and the only Chinese restaurant for miles, Dai's had become their ritual, smack in the middle of the school week, when Eddie and Emily would be ripe with complaints.

"That sounds like a tough place to be in," Jon told Eddie, who was annoyed at a classmate who'd taken credit for the group's work.

"That must have been disappointing," he consoled Emily, who was bummed she hadn't made second chair in cello.

That was it? I thought. Wait. That *was* it. Kids didn't always want their problems solved; sometimes they just wanted an ear—and to be validated. Jon was excellent at it, I noticed, as they sighed, feeling heard, and moved on.

Actually, I noticed, he was kind of good at everything.

One Saturday night, as we all lounged about in the den, I told Jon that I really believed that he was a bonafide genius.

"You think this dumb ass is genius?" said Eddie, looking up from a marathon of *World of Warcraft*.

"He's smart," Emily said, setting down her bow after a

two-hour practice. "But I don't know if I'd, like, call him a genius or anything. No offense, Dad."

I stroked Jon's goatee. "Well, your dad's a genius to me."

"Let's find out," Eddie said. His fingers clacked away on the keyboard as he forwarded Jon an online Mensa quiz.

"Eddie, come on," Jon resisted, with as much fight as a world-class arm wrestler would exert after being challenged to a match with a grandmother. Five minutes later, Jon aced 150, just ten points below Einstein's 160.

"Your turn." Jon forwarded it to me.

"Nah, I'm good," I said.

"What do you mean, 'you're good'? Doesn't everyone want to know her IQ?"

I didn't. Not with one certified and two potential geniuses in the room. It was a little intimidating, but I was cornered, so I painstakingly answered all the questions on the test. My score came in at a surprising 135, which put me in the "Gifted" category. Heck, maybe I wasn't such a dumb ass, even if Eddie and Emily were quick to remind us both that it was just an online test.

Maybe I belonged with this group, it occurred to me that night, as I stayed over for the first time with the kids there, taking one step closer to becoming part of this instant family. Love wasn't just about the two beings in the center of the picture; it was also about affecting and making connections with those around them.

What was it the kids could learn from me? What could I be to them? I wasn't sure yet, seeing as they were both so together. But somehow it felt like another piece of the puzzle had snapped into place.

Still, the next morning, as we made blueberry scones, I wondered if this all wasn't just a little too perfect. Would conflict rear itself when his ex-wife came to get the kids?

She was sweeter than pie as she shook my hand and told

me it was great to meet me. We talked for a bit while the kids gathered their stuff. She was personable, self-assured, and could spin a funny tale. I liked hearing about bunion surgeries she performed, toenail medication she prescribed, and other tales from the hospital where she interned. In some sisterly way I liked, too, her story of going back to school to reinvent herself. Most especially though, I liked how non-threatening she seemed as she asked about our night and then brought up to Jon a tuition installment due to Emily's orchestra program. Clearly, their once best friend relationship had been distilled down to an evolved adult friendship which revolved around managing their kids, which was impressive in light of my divorced friends' issues.

Her only tangible flaw seemed to be bad judgment; after all, she had divorced this incredible man. Although Jon had told me the divorce had been mutual, I learned at some point that it had been she who had served him with the papers.

Insanity, if there was ever a clearer definition of the word.

I met his mother next. *Snap, snap, snap,* went more puzzle pieces. Harriet Ginzberg clapped her hands to my cheeks. "I don't know what it is, but you look like a Siegel." Tears rimmed her huge blue eyes.

I know a lot of women who might have squirmed in that situation. The presumptuous comment, the endless emotion pouring from those mini oceans for eyes, the potential for Jewish smothering. But it worked like a charm for me, and so I offered it back. "I know what you mean," I said. "I kind of feel like one." And she nearly fell over, *verklempt.*

"Welcome." Jon's stepfather Stan hugged me heartily to his short, sturdy frame; at seventy-eight-years-old, he was still built like a bull. His white Santa mustache smashed into my cheek as I hugged him back.

On the trip home from New Jersey, Jon apologized. "Unless you stop them, they'll tell you the same stories, over and over."

"Well, they're new to me."

The only thing I felt truly bad about was that I couldn't reciprocate the warm welcome. When I told my dad that I'd met the love of my life his response had been, *I'll meet him when I meet him.*

"He sounds like a character," Jon had said.

"A character from *Six Feet Under* meets the *Walking Dead.*"

"Still?"

But I had given him the editorial already about my father's flatline personality—and my lifelong quest to understand what had first jaded him: his own less than perfect childhood, my mother's death, or a career of burying the dead. Forget celebrating our own events, we had to drag him to his own Father's Day brunches. The only things that still seemed to excite him were finding some good herb, as he liked to call his marijuana, being intimate with his newest lady, and caring for his cats. I understood that last part, although he did push the envelope, even for my standards. *I can't come to dinner. Milo has a cough. He needs me.*

At least my siblings were happy to go on a triple date and meet for themselves the guy who I not only was "moving so fast with" but "idolizing."

"I mean, who is this guy—God?" my sister Jasmine had teased me.

"Seriously," my brother Greg agreed. "Am I meeting a mortal or the son of Zeus?"

And yet, just a week after sharing with Jon an evening of family-style baked clams and shrimp parmesan at their favorite restaurant, their phone calls started coming in.

"Can you ask Jon what he thinks?" Jasmine said. "Should I extend my fifteen-year mortgage to a thirty-year, or double up on payments and get it over with?"

"Is Jon there?" Greg asked. "I want to know what he thinks of this stock…also, can you ask him how he interprets this lease clause?"

"Oh, hello, by the way," I joked, but I liked that they called. And I liked that Jon treated their calls with the same intensity and importance as his work calls.

He was flattered and happy to connect with them. Having siblings ask for his opinion was not something he was accustomed to; he barely spoke to his brother and sister, though he didn't seem to want to elaborate on what the tensions had been about over the years.

I didn't press him, although I couldn't possibly imagine what their gripes might be.

I guessed some people were just crazy.

"Don't gaze into each other's eyes looking for meaning. Look outward together."

- *J.O., Elmont, married twelve years*

KINGDOMS

Two months later, I rented out my Cape-style house to a young couple in medical school and moved into the Poltergeist complex.

Merging the royal décor with my eclectic, country farm-house-style was no easy decorating feat, but with a little yel-low-cream paint (to cancel out the stone colored walls), things brightened up. I reupholstered the navy, gold-tasseled silk chairs in chocolate faux-suede, swapped out the 150-pound sterling silver elephant and its marble pedestal for a plant, switched out some ornate throw rugs and bedding for more casual prints, traded the banquet linens and settings from the dining room table for a wooden bowl of realistic fruit, and suggested that we sell the throne on eBay.

Jon spun on his heel. "What? I thought you liked that chair?"

I liked that he'd thought enough of himself to purchase it; I liked that he seemed like a regular-size human sitting on it, but even he had to admit it wasn't doing much to warm up the place. "Don't you think that corner would look great with a comfy armchair in a bright print?"

"It has to stay." He straddled a tone between commanding and begging. "Come on, you've had your way with the place. Let me put my foot down on this one."

It was true I'd taken a lot of liberties. It was also true that things could be worse. So my boyfriend had a throne. Arguably, it was better than a La-Z-Boy.

In exchange for my capitulation, he agreed to let me keep my monstrous juicer and its accoutrements on the counter-top. Before me, his kitchen had been showroom tidy. Even the insides of his cabinets had been organized as if their contents were for sale. All spice labels faced outward. All like foods went together. The new chaos of my mismatched vitamins, protein powders, shakers, and measuring cups seemed to compromise his aesthetic sense.

"You're really going to put vitamins with the canned goods?" he said, aghast.

"Well, there's no other cabinet with extra space at this point. Besides, it's good for you to challenge your OCD," I lovingly told him as I jammed in the last golden glass bottle and heaved the door closed. "It might even cure you."

"I don't have OCD."

"Are you sure about that?" I threw my arms around his neck. "I think I know of a potato chip bag or two that would beg to differ."

"All right," he said, tickled, and also (kind of) admitting, if not to the actual disorder found in the *Diagnostic and Statistical Manual of Mental Disorders,* then to having some kind of issue with detail management. After all, it wasn't every man who would finish a bag to the last crumb, relieve it of all air molecules, then fold it neatly into origami.

Then there was the garbage routine.

"You can't be serious," he'd laughed the week before, holding up a shoebox I had deposited, whole, into the garbage. "This takes up the entire bag. All you have to do is this." He dropped the box to the ground, stomped on it, folded it into two—then two again—wrapped a rubber band around it, and then dropped it back into the trash.

I saw his point. Still. "You know I will *never* do that, right?"

"I'll make a deal with you." He scooped me into his arms. "If you can't do it, then leave it for me. I'll do it."

"Deal." It was nice having a man who wanted to take out the garbage. It was even nicer to be able to point out our differences to each other in a loving, affectionate way. What could go wrong so long as we communicated?

Our opposing food cultures was another one of those fun chasms between us, and we communicated about it plenty. He liked meat, and I liked tofu. Well, nobody really likes tofu, I conceded, but I liked the idea of plant-based protein, and so I tolerated tofu.

He liked grease, fat, butter, oils, and cream. I liked vegetable purees, broths, and soy creamer. Well, nobody really likes soy creamer, I also admitted, but when you're trying not to eat dairy, soy creamer is a tolerable substitute.

Setting down a plate of braised tempeh before him, I would giggle inside. But he was a good sport, and so long as a plate was set in front of him, he was happy; he liked being served. And here I surprised myself to learn that I liked serving him.

Middle-child syndrome was at least partly responsible for my need to please. But mainly, I loved seeing his face light up when I set down food, especially when I'd succumbed and prepared something greasy or cheesy, like penne a la vodka, the "mac daddy" of gastrointestinal distress, which his kids also loved. He would laugh at my hesitation as I brought a forkful to my lips.

"It's just a bowl of pasta, Heather!"

He thought people could eat whatever they wanted, because he could eat whatever he wanted. If I ate a porterhouse steak, I would need to go to the hospital, I told him. He thought I was kidding until one Saturday, he convinced me to eat two slices of pizzeria pizza—which, of course, I did—and I needed a two-hour nap afterward, not to mention the emergency visit to the dermatologist for a phototherapy treatment, during which I stood naked in a vertical tanning bed of sorts, lined with narrow-band, non-tanning UVB bulbs.

"What does your dermatologist say about your diet?" Jon asked when I came home, crisped and sizzling, the red spots even angrier from the attack of artificial ultraviolet rays.

"He doesn't believe diet plays any role in the health of my skin," I said, changing into soft, silky pajama pants.

"So…you don't believe him?"

"No, it's that I know from personal experience." I motioned to my legs. "If I eat something inflammatory, like tomatoes, my skin goes haywire."

"Heath," he said sweetly. "Don't you think *just maybe* there are other variables to consider besides tomatoes? I mean, how about lack of sleep, or…cat dander…or pollen…or any other factor? Besides, what's so horrible about tomatoes?"

"Well, besides being a nightshade vegetable, which are terrible for inflammation—that's why arthritics are advised not to eat them—tomatoes have tomatine in them."

"What the hell is tomatine?" He exploded into laughter.

"Tomatine is a natural toxin that people with compromised immune systems can't deal with. Listen, trust me on this. Eating cleanly helps my skin."

Jon had never heard of many of the books I had read, like *The China Study*, touted as the "most comprehensive study of nutrition and health ever conducted," and which basically states that if more than twenty percent of a person's diet is from animal products, he or she is "turning on" cancer cells. Also, Andrew Weil, M.D.'s *Eating Well for Optimum Health*, which discusses the anti-inflammatory diet.

"I don't know, Heath. There has to be a better way. If millions of people have this, someone has to be working toward a cure. Is there really no pill you can take?"

There was in fact a shot I could get, an innocuous term for a biological injection that would basically shut down my immune system so that my skin would stop replicating itself, but the side effects—cancer, Hepatitis B, heart failure, nervous system problems—scared the hell out of me and weren't worth the possible "seventy-five percent clearance rate." It was never one hundred percent clearance, and it was never, of course, guaranteed. So light treatments and topical creams were the lesser of the evils, I told him—as were diet restrictions.

"Trust me," I said. "If I could live on a diet of martinis and Doritos with no effect, I'd be in heaven. But I know better."

"Well, if you say so, I believe you." He kissed my battered arm. I knew he didn't really believe me, but that was okay. I had lived with Psoriasis since I was a teenager—and knew all there was to know about it. Didn't I? Maybe. But it might be nice to find that pill if it existed.

I began to question other things I thought I knew—like my fear of electromagnetic energy from televisions. Where *had* I read about that? Certainly not in one of the scientific journals Jon subscribed to. I would giggle at my former self, the person gullible enough to believe something she'd read once *somewhere,* as we settled in to watch the evening news together. And why not face the dark reality of the world, anyway? Who was I really helping to hide from it? Not myself, when I stood clueless at a party, not knowing what the hell everyone was talking about.

I felt myself stripping away pretenses, too. By month four, I'd traded down my cute tank top nighties for old T-shirts. He'd swapped his contact lenses for his glasses during our television hour. I let my kinky curly hair air dry. He left the bathroom door open while he used the toilet—which I corrected him on. No one needs to see that; I don't care how comfortable you are together.

Around our fifth-month anniversary, one of Jon's long-shot hedge funds showed promise. This was his chance to regain his footing. He paced the den, pitching a hotel development project, rattling off financial terms I'd never heard of, and asking for sums of money that seemed laughable. Meanwhile, I'd been having a hard time displaying tabletop rack cards for our musicians that read "$1.00 artist donation fee *suggested.*"

He hung up the phone, collapsed on the couch next to me, and sighed. "I don't know if I'm ever going to pull this off."

"Are you kidding?" I put down my laptop, where I'd been

creating a new flyer for Tarot Card readings. My whole spiel to myself about being positive, aiming for a goal, and taking action seemed like a micro version of his thinking. "I've never heard anyone dream so big. Or ask point-blank for money like that. If anyone can raise money for these projects, it's you."

"You really think so?"

Was he kidding? "I *know* so."

He lit up and went back to the phone.

Within a month, he had raised most of the money for one of the projects—the development of an eco-luxe hotel with private condos on a small island in Turks and Caicos—and needed to travel to raise the rest of the money.

"You have to come with me." He grasped my hand as if I might float away. I grasped back, unable to fathom even a day, let alone a week, where I might not be in the same room as him. "Plus you can bring your writing," he said.

My writing. The MFA degree now hung on my wall of accomplishments—Jon had come to the ceremony. But who could focus on that half-baked manuscript that loomed on my desktop, in its unfinished, unwieldy state?

There is a time for writing and a time for living, I'd scribbled in my journal, and then slammed it shut.

We began to travel together—to Vail, San Francisco, Miami—and back and forth to Turks and Caicos so often, it began to feel like a home away from home, which, serendipitously, was the closest thing to a cure for my skin as anything.

We would rent an SUV, I'd drop Jon at the office, and after I was good and seared and crisped, I'd find my way around the island—to the airport, the IGA supermarket. I'd pick him up for lunch, and we'd go to The Conch Shack, where the large shells were plucked from the ocean, and, much to my dismay, the poor creatures from inside fried instantaneously into Cracked Conch.

We stayed in Providenciales, the heart of Turks and Caicos

tourism, with its strip of boutique and brand hotels along a pristine white beach with aqua water as unreal as the magic marker color. Provo, as it was called, operated like a small rural town. When we climbed down the plane steps, with its railing hot to the touch in the bright white heat, we were greeted by the airport attendant who also moonlighted as a bartender at our favorite local restaurant. We made friends with hotel staff and restaurant owners—"Belongers" was the official term for citizens of Turks and Caicos, which cracked me up. I mean, what a way to make visitors feel like outsiders.

"Welcome back, Mr. and Mrs. Siegel," they would say, and we would squeeze hands, not bothering to correct them.

"You're becoming a jet-setter," my coffeehouse friends said, jealously. I laughed. Me? A jetsetter? But I was travelling on a jet. And my life was broadening. The coffeehouse girl in me, and maybe before her, the foster girl I'd once been—the one who wore hand-me-downs and shared bathwater to save her foster mother money—felt a little guilty about the plane fare and missing work. But vaguely, I was aware that a new ten-year cycle had begun. And maybe there was something to the rabbi's lecture that still lingered in my mind: the idea that when two halves are joined, they can make a dent in the world together.

After a few months of back and forth, a small development team was created—which I saw as a version of the movie *Ocean's 11* in which each character has a unique talent but instead of eleven men, Jon's team was comprised of five. The two original members, the project owners—a British ex-pat turned Belonger, who was in construction, and an Atlanta millionaire, who was in development—happened to also have backgrounds as engineers, and they felt a kinship toward Jon.

One night at a brainstorming dinner, the Brit arranged three glasses of water in close proximity to each other, handed Jon three butter knives and asked Jon to "build a bridge" between the glasses. The layman's move—the one I was masterminding in my head—would be to try and make a triangle out of the butter knives, but the glasses were just far enough away from each other that the butter knives would not reach from glass to glass. Jon squinted and, five seconds later, constructed an overlapping connection between the knives to build the bridge.

The Brit leapt from the table and threw down his napkin. "I've been showing that trick at dinner for twenty years," he cried. "And you're the first person to ever get it right."

They asked Jon to join the team as CFO. I was proud of him and saw why he'd passed on my imaginary coffeehouse CEO idea. He wasn't any schlepp, and those people in the top echelon of engineering and hotel development knew it.

"Don't sell yourself short," Jon told me, complimenting how I helped the conversations flow and made people feel at ease; how was it that I always knew how to rescue someone floundering in an uncomfortable silence?

Did I? If I did, we could thank Dale Carnegie for that trick. *How to Win Friends and Influence People* had resonated with me when I'd read it in college. "What's the most beautiful music to someone's ears? The sound of his or her own name," Carnegie wrote. But I was also genuinely interested. It was exciting to break out and meet people who were doing fascinating things with their lives. The only thing that still gnawed at me was the price of the dinner bill at the end of each night that made me cringe in a *I need to start tithing ten percent of my salary again* kind of way.

"It's more than that," Jon said one night as we snuggled in the hotel room. "You heard Karl."

Karl was an investor with whom Jon had negotiated firmly, and who finally gave in to Jon's terms. He'd toasted one night in celebration. *To Heather, when I met you, I knew Jon had to be a good guy underneath all that tough negotiating.*

"Well, I wouldn't want to be pitted against you either," I said.

"The good news is you never have to. We're a team." He grew teary-eyed. "I just wish I could have met you earlier. I'm mad we didn't get to spend our youth together, too."

"We wouldn't have been ready for each other."

He nodded. We didn't even need to say the obvious: that while he was in college doing complex engineering math and courting his first wife, I was in eighth grade vying for a badminton championship and trying to memorize the formula for the Pythagorean Theorem; or that even just a few years before we'd met, we still wouldn't have been ready. My vegetarian-cult-self and his non-quasi-humbled, yet-to-have-career-disappointment-stockbroking-self would have clashed. We'd needed to evolve to this point in time before we were perfectly suited. Maybe this is what the rabbi had meant when he talked about "meriting" meeting a soulmate.

"We have the rest of our lives to make up for it," I said.

The beauty of finding your true counterpart is being able to reach into the past and present and see an infinite design, I'd written in my journal then. Oh, Heather.

Eight months to the day we had met at Starbucks, he got down on his knee and proposed to me during a Caribbean sunset that was both as beautiful as a Monet painting and as gooey as the inside of a Cadbury Caramel.

"You would make me the happiest man in the world if you would say yes," he said.

"Of course, yes!"

Then he opened a box to reveal a ring that could have easily been mistaken for one inside a Cracker Jack box.

"Is that real?"

"Is it okay that I want to show the world how much I love you?"

Later, when I met up with my girlfriends, they saw all right—dollar signs, and it made me really uncomfortable.

"Holy shit! Figures you would get this ring," my childhood friend Siggy said with a laugh, knowing how little I knew about diamonds and jewelry. "That's got to be at least four carats."

"Five," Jon told me when I asked him.

"*Really?*"

"Are you seriously complaining that your diamond is too big? You want me to get a smaller one?"

"That would be too weird, right?"

"Heather!"

"All right, all right. It's good. It's great! *Thank you.*"

Still, I would stare at the ring on my finger as if it were a planet, in the sunlight and in the shade, studying its depth and sparkle.

Sometimes, as we jetted back and forth, I would twist it around my finger and make a fist to hold it in my palm, away from the judgmental gaze of passersby—or worse, potential muggers—and I would secretly wish that it was just a teensy weensy less conspicuous. That's when the recurring nightmare began. I would be in the supermarket, and I'd look down and the stone would be gone from the setting.

Was it a nightmare or a premonition?

"Unlike most people I don't think marriage is a compromise. I think it's a partnership where both people are equal; they may contribute different things, but they are equal partners working together."

- A. W., Upper Brookville, married twenty years

"A marriage isn't 50/50, it's 100/100."

- J. D., Locust Valley, married sixteen years

NAMESAKE

We planned our wedding, visiting the usual banquet halls on Long Island. Of the two million plus weddings that take place every year in the U.S., I wouldn't have been surprised if one million were held at Leonard's of Great Neck. We passed on that venue, as well as the historic Lessings' properties set on rolling fields of green, and even The Crescent, a huge hall on the rocky north shore beach, where I found to my surprise a picture of my ex and his wife hanging on the paneled wall of bridal fame. Nothing felt quite like us—two excited people ready to share with the world their remarkable, metaphysical love that needed to be honored and not churned through a wedding machine, which is how in the end, we decided that only a destination wedding in Turks and Caicos would do, with fifty of our friends and family flying in for a three-day weekend. Most were thrilled, some secretly wished we weren't so insistent on proving how remarkable our love was.

I found a strapless dress that J-Lo would have worn—at least that's what the savvy sales ladies at Meika dress shop in Woodbury convinced me of as I stepped out of the dressing room, wearing an ivory white design with what looked like Desert Flowers, seen in the beach gardens of Turks and Caicos, blossoming up the torso.

I had never really imagined myself as a bride, but maybe,

if forced at knifepoint, I could have summoned a vision of myself wearing white combat boots and a long white Tuxedo jacket with a mini-skirt. But that cool and edgy persona was blurring before my eyes—and why not? Flowers weren't so terrible. They were actually sort of…beautiful.

Still, when I hooked up with the popular local wedding officiant of the Christian faith, the recognized religion of the island, and reviewed his one-pager replete with "man and wife" and promises "to honor God's guidance by his Spirit through the Word," I paused.

This was not only not me, but also, not us. But what was? Jon hadn't been to a temple since his son's bar mitzvah. And a Kabbalastic wedding seemed forced. Slowly, I'd been losing interest in attending those courses. Back in New York, I'd taken Jon to one and honestly couldn't help giggling at his flabbergasted reaction. It was almost as bad as when he'd attended my friend's baby-naming in Brooklyn, and we'd sat cross-legged for an hour in a group circle, listening to chanting, before the host asked us to help lift up "the circle of good wishes." (Jon obliged, pulling up the imaginary ring, but also leading the charge and hoisting it overhead. "Well, someone had to get that thing off the ground!" he would tell me afterward in the car.) I think, in part, this had to do with my coming to the slow realization that knowledge of spirituality meant nothing if one didn't practice it. I mean, what good is the yogi doing if she leaves class and flips the bird to someone who cuts her off in the parking lot?

What we needed for our vows, I decided, what I was look-ing for, was a secular text we could then infuse with our own unique viewpoints on marriage, viewpoints that I realized, after skimming state documents, could be anything, so long as we were of age, not already married, not marrying a rela-tive, and had U.S. birth certificates.

If we wanted leprechauns as ringbearers, so be it. If we wanted to marry for revenge, kicks, or friendship, it was our choice. Obviously, marriage is as much a private, personal choice, as it is a civil, legal union, but I was surprised to see that there was no form per se that I could pluck from the files of Town Hall that *defined* marriage other than by its legality.

There was lots of information I reviewed about the history of marriage, not the least of which, even in Western culture, had to do with the oppression of women, the bolstering of men's economic and political status, and, mind-bogglingly, the current oppression against same-sex couples (the Marriage Equality Act wouldn't be passed into law until 2011).

"Listen to this," I would call to Jon, reading him more mind-blowing facts, such as up until the nineteenth century in the U.S., a wife's legal personality was covered under her husband's. This meant that she could not own property, make a will, earn her own money, engage in contracts, or leave her husband without his consent. "Or this," I would call, explaining that it would take until the 1970s for the law to lift restrictions on divorce (through the birth of no-fault divorce).

"Crazy," Jon agreed, handing me a cup of tea I hadn't asked for, but he knew I'd want. We, I decided then, were equal partners who, with or without a government form, wanted to take our love ride to its highest height in a public solidification of our love trinity.

And since no document existed to explain that, I cobbled one together, pulling bits and pieces, including—why not?—the "together we are gathered on this day" line to put the officiant at ease. While I was at it, I wove in some text from *The New Jewish Wedding*, a book Harriet had given me as an engagement present—her way of asking her daughter-in-law-to-be for *some* kind of Judaism in our unconventional ceremony. How could I say no to a woman who was so enthusiastic for us?

We'd called with the good news the weekend we'd gotten engaged, and Harriet had started bawling. "Oh, I just can't stand it, I'm so excited! Stan, honey, pick up the phone! Stanny? Where the heck is he? Stanley! Are you picking up?"

"I'm already here, Harriet. What is—" His voice cut off as he dropped the phone. "Hello? Hello? What is it, Harriet?"

"Stan, honey, we have an engagement party to throw! Oh, I just can't stand it!"

And they had thrown us a party. Driven down from Cherry Hill, New Jersey, with their car loaded with "good" platters, an old coffee maker from the 70s in its original packaging, crackers bought two cases for the price of one, a round of brie that was on sale at Wegmans with baked figs inside— something Harriet had engineered herself—and scores of brownies, muffins, and seven-layer bars she had prepared a month in advance, labeled and frozen.

She was big on baking and even bigger on freezing. Bagels shaped in the form of turkeys were set out for breakfast in May. Chicken from July was served in December. Stan had, of course, wrapped all the goods with his signature four-layer technique: Saran Wrap to lock out the oxygen, followed by tin foil, twisted into a plastic bag, sealed with masking tape, and topped with a final layer of Saran Wrap.

Perhaps where Jon had picked up a technique or two?

"Not a chance," Jon said, straightening up the countertops and taking out the trash after they'd gone to bed, their paper trail driving him batty. "And listen, it's sweet that you indulge them, but don't feel obligated to use that book my mother gave you. It's really not that important to me." He'd had the full-blown traditional wedding once, he told me, and, all planning aside, being barefoot on the beach and saying "I do" seemed more authentic to him than anything.

I agreed but also explained that I *wanted* to please my mother-in-law-to-be. Besides, it wasn't as if she'd handed me the Old Testament to work with. A little Jewish touch to an otherwise spiritual ceremony seemed as innocuous to me as leaving five bucks under Emily's pillow to keep up the Tooth

Fairy tale—not that she still believed; she finally confessed to having read the truth years earlier in a children's book of all places—but there was certainly no harm in *not* offending someone who did believe.

Harriet was beyond thrilled to hear, and in the months leading up to the wedding, she called constantly, updating me on the beach dress she'd found for herself and the wine glasses she'd located for the blessing over the wine.

I hadn't actually incorporated a blessing and wine, but, again, how could I say no to her when it meant so very much to her and so very little to me? Just as I wasn't against giving her and Stan a speaking part during that blessing or walking seven circles around Jon and he around me—even if in my heart of hearts I didn't even believe in the seven days of creation that this circling was supposed to symbolize.

"Was that my mom *again*?" Jon asked.

"At least she's showing interest," I said. When I'd told my father that we were getting married in the Caribbean, he'd huffed and puffed about the inconvenience of it all.

"Sorry," Jon said. "Did he get his plane ticket yet?"

"Jasmine got it for him, and Greg promised me he'd drive him to the airport."

"Well, that's good. Meanwhile, the crazy part is he'll probably enjoy himself."

Jon had started to really get a handle on my father, seeing for himself his desensitized personality. But Jon also admitted that my dad was kind of hard not to like and understood how I'd forgiven him for his shortcomings. When he got out of his own way, he could be a really friendly guy, a kind soul, a cool cat who my childhood friends had once called the Count for his slicked-back ponytail, goatee, and funereal suits. And he not only loved to party but liked to get the people around him "wrecked"—his favorite term.

I made a mental note to keep him away from Harriet and Stan.

We flew down to the island with our immediate family a few days before the ceremony, thinking it would be fun to spend some time with everyone before the extended group arrived.

"You guys want to go straight in the water?" Jon and I asked the family when the airport van dropped us at the hotel. "It's beautiful out."

The kids were hot and tired. Harriet and Stan had some serious unpacking to do. Jasmine and Greg wanted to work out. And my dad—and his new girlfriend—wanted to score some weed from a Belonger.

Jon and I padded down to the water. It was still lunchtime, and the beach felt abandoned, save for the towels and sunhats and paperback novels left behind to guard chairs. We stripped down to our suits. We were pros at taking the three-hour flight by now. We'd brought carry-ons, worn our suits under our clothes, and advised everyone else to do the same. Why anyone would want to go jogging, or unpack, or nap when they could be here on the beach, reveling in the sunshine was beyond me. Jon seemed to read my thoughts as we lay in the sun holding hands, eyes closed, enjoying the moment.

"They're crazy," he said.

"Right?" I could feel the sun's rays penetrating my sensitive skin.

"Your skin looks good by the way," he said, again getting inside my head. He smoothed a hand over my arm. "Totally clear."

"I've been noticing that lately. It's the clearest it's ever been. You must be my cure."

"I think I am."

"I'm not even kidding."

"Neither am I."

He was beautiful, lying there in the sun with his bristly goatee. His English Lithuanian skin was already browning, curly brown chest hairs darkening, freckles disappearing as the skin around them tanned. I felt like I had been eating peanuts my whole life, thinking they were great, until someone delivered me chocolate-covered almonds. I felt like the luckiest woman alive to be holding hands with him on this beach. Marrying him. Hello, husband.

Jon lifted his glasses and looked at me. "Did you say something?" I laughed. I was going to have to be careful with this telepathy in the future, especially with birthday presents and surprises.

"Hey, you know what we should do?" I said, having a sudden brainstorm. "We should do a michveh."

I explained how I had done one at the Kabbalah center once, with my sister, many years earlier, during our brainwashing time. The two of us had gotten naked and dipped ourselves in a small pool, dunking under water several times, saying blessings to cleanse ourselves of past mistakes and impurities. It seemed silly at the time, and maybe sillier as I recounted the tale to Jon, but hell, if we were going to do wine blessings, what could it hurt?

"Okay," Jon said. "But how?"

"Supposedly the ocean is a natural michveh," I continued.

"Well, I am hot," he said.

Once we were in, I explained the caveat. "Now you have to strip," I said.

"You mean a flimsy piece of nylon is going to block me from becoming pure?"

"Just do it." I unhooked my bikini top. Five or six people floated a few yards to our left, a safe enough distance away. Jon hedged, then took off his trunks. I took off my bottoms.

"Now what?" He laughed. I giggled too. It was freeing.

"Now we have to dunk under water, and every time we do, we have to imagine ourselves washing away our past."

Jon dipped and bobbed up, and I did the same, sliding down beneath the crystalline surface and pushing my toes off the soft sand, back up for air. We kept doing it until we were giddy and breathless, our tongues salted. The sun was high. The sky cloudless. And suddenly I felt primordial, as if connected to the first man and woman on earth, as if at home in the ocean, naked, with my man. And for the first time in my life I understood why people wanted to have children, to clone themselves. It was to make more of *this*.

"Tell me you don't feel different," I said, throwing my arms around his neck.

"I don't know what just happened but I feel incredible."

We hugged for a long time, swaying in the bobbing water, slow dancing, as the resort—the world—disappeared. It was just us. "I do," I said, practicing my line.

"I do too," he said, kissing me. Off in the distance I could hear far-off voices, water breaking, a speedboat zipping by, the sounds of civilization calling us back to shore.

"We should probably put our bathing suits back on," he said.

"Just one more dunk," I lied, seeing what was heading his way. I took his shorts. He closed his eyes and dipped under water. I pulled on my bottoms discreetly and swam away.

"Hey!" Jon yelled, understanding what was happening as my dad backstroked over in his black bikini.

"This place is fucking paradise, isn't it, Jon?"

"We knew you'd love it. Heath! Get back here!"

It was the beginning of sunset; the sky streaked pink as Jasmine and Emily walked me toward the steps that led to the beach. The three of us sank our feet into the cool white sand. My dress flowed, my soft updo loosened in the wind, a few flowers came undone.

Jon stood barefoot on the shore, wearing white pants and a pink button-up shirt opened to mid-chest.

He was already mine, I knew. But who didn't like a show?

We walked circles around each other, getting dizzy, and

laughing at the silliness of it. Under the makeshift chuppah his construction buddy had built, Harriet and Stan "ba-ruched" and "adonaid." "Bashert," someone in the front row said. And we said our vows, topping our already perfect cake with a sun-kissed cherry while everyone, believing in this beautiful narrative, cried—including the Count.

This isn't to say there weren't any glitches. The wedding official had pronounced me the husband and Jon the wife. There was also the moment two days before the ceremony, when, during a surprise beach party, Jon's work friends had thrown us on the undeveloped island, my engagement ring hurtled off my finger and into the abyss of white powdery sand.

Jon had been on a boat snorkeling, about twenty feet out from a volleyball match. I'd been drinking rum punches in the hot sun, growing fiercely competitive about the game, when I tapped the ball into the air, and someone from the other team yelled, "Something just flew off…"

The planet had gone into orbit. And then everything slowed as I fell to my knees and searched, hands and feet all around me crushing and overturning the sand.

Jon sensed from the boat that something was wrong, but by the time he docked, the area flanking the net had been ravaged.

"First of all, we have insurance," he said. "Second of all, don't read into this."

Too late. Although the truth was I wasn't thinking that losing the ring was, say, some kind of omen or a harbin-ger of bad things to come. I'd actually been thinking about judgment again, the evil eye I'd been getting about the ring, even from those who lovingly ribbed me about its size. Also, my lack of ownership; I was still secretly wearing it as if it belonged to someone else. Had I subconsciously wanted it to be lost?

Everyone was pitching in by then, but as they dug and

churned the sand over, the more hopeless it began to seem. Jon and his engineer buddies asked everyone to step back, then lined us up; we moved forward in straight lines, together on our hands and knees, sifting through individual columns of sand. After an hour of valiant effort, the mosquitoes swarmed in, the sky darkened, and we were forced to leave.

We docked on the main island and sent everyone back to the hotel. Eddie, Emily, Jon, and I drove to a local restaurant where we borrowed a metal detector from the owner.

"Don't worry," Eddie said. "We'll find it in the morning."

After twenty passes and not a single beep, Jon said, "Or not," and we all laughed—me to the point of tears.

"Wow, you're both really being a really good sport about this," Emily said.

"Well," I said, trying to absorb Jon's attitude, "it's just a ring. Right, Jon?"

"Right," Jon said. And then the crack: "But, I mean, it would be nice to find it!"

That night I dreamt of the ring sparkling in the sand and imagined all the evil eye being cleansed by the stars and the moon, the negativity dissipating into the air.

Okay, I'm really ready to wear it, I whispered in my dream, knowing that I—the person who had been resisting this new and different lifestyle of first class and fancy dinners—was saying more.

When I woke, I knew Jon would find the ring, and that its energy would be different.

And if it wasn't cleansed?

Oh well. I guess I'd suck it up, get over my weird bullshit, and deal with the burden of having to wear a nice ring.

The next day, Jon and Eddie returned to the hotel beach with sunken shoulders. As they made their way toward me, I felt terrible for Jon and for being such a spoiled idiot for having anything other than appreciation toward his gift.

"Sorry," I mouthed as he approached. He nodded, then

held up his hand and showed me the planet sparkling on his pinkie.

The metal detector had been useless after all; it had been found by an honest waiter sifting through the sand, he told me as he slid it onto my finger.

"It feels different," I said. "Lighter."

Jon quickly checked the side baguettes and sighed, relieved to find that no physical changes could be detected.

We returned to New York and got married a second time. Turns out we weren't the only ones who considered our Turks and Caicos wedding a formality to our love.

"This is a license from where?" the motor vehicles clerk wanted to know. "Turkey?"

"Fuck it," Jon said, running into the same walls as me when dealing with a health insurance agent when he tried to add me to the policy. "It's not worth the brain damage. We need to be recognized by the State of New York."

We suited up into our costumes again a few days later, pulled Emily and Eddie from their classes, and dragged them down to the county clerk with us, then out to the beach in Oyster Bay for a quick ceremony with a town official and a lunch of fried shrimp at the Canterbury Ale house.

They slunk down in their seats. "Don't you guys want to change?"

"Nah, we'll get free dessert this way," Jon said.

I cleaved to his side and embraced my new step-monster role. "Jon, maybe we can even get them to play our song?"

I didn't think that changing my name would be a big deal, but somehow it actually was. I would sign my name over and over—back at motor vehicles, or on credit card applications—aware that something was shifting. I was now Mrs. Siegel, part of the Siegel clan, no longer a single entity in the world. I liked my name with a Mrs. in front.

I had never really thought about it up until those weeks,

but once I was married, some basic part of me finally admitted to craving a sense of traditionalism in my life. Granted, I knew that tradition to me meant something quite different to, say, the radical feminist—taking the man's name traditionally went back to that awful history of marriage, in which the woman had no identity other than "Mrs."

But to me, swapping out my surname meant matriculating into the mainstream and leaving the fringe behind—as well as the fractured family from which I'd come.

Still, a few months after we got married, I moved forward with the choice to open my second store. I chose the sleepy, somewhat depressed town of Lindenhurst, a far cry from San Diego, but a place that seemed to be begging for culture, or at least something other than a Subway or Quiznos. And it was a place where I could channel more of who I'd become as a restaurateur.

It took almost a year to turn my blueprints into reality. And two months after opening, I felt like I had made my point to myself. The answer, I knew as I looked around the bustling room on a Friday night, candles aglow, music streaming, customers chowing down on healthy salads, our first review—a thumbs up from a *Newsday* food critic—framed on the wall, and thank you notes in the email book (Thank you for taking a chance on this town!) was: yes, my ideas were still relevant. And then I would check my watch, counting the minutes down until I could be back at home, cozy wozy, sharing some Ben & Jerry's and watching a movie with my newlywed.

I still enjoyed the physicality of the restaurant business, the soreness in my calves and feet after a particularly heavy rush, and the sense of accomplishment that came with unspiking the night's tickets and tallying the register. But I was kidding myself if I didn't confess that staying out until 1:00 a.m. or 2:00 a.m. on a weekend night had lost some appeal. Even when Jon came to visit, the night seemed endless. When he would leave around midnight, I'd feel imprisoned.

"Just throwing it out there," Jon said one night as I crawled in bed next to him. "But would you ever think about selling the stores?"

"I don't know. I mean, as much as they have become a pain, I do still love them."

"Your call."

I lay my head on his chest, my husband, the one person in the world who now had not only my back, but my best interests in mind—and vice versa. "Why, you think I should?"

"Well," he tucked his hands under his neck. "Honestly. I think you don't need the hassle anymore. You have me—us."

My eyes traveled down a patch of moonlight and to the seahorse painting we'd been given as a wedding gift by Jon's colleague, whose wife had painted the piece. The eight inch by eleven inch picture of two beautiful brown and gold seahorses entwining in the sea had come with a card with some interesting facts. Seahorses are monogamous. They mate for life and rarely go anywhere without each other.

As much as I wanted to be home with Jon all day while he worked from home—entwining in the sea—the thought of doing nothing unnerved me, as it always had. It was a by-product of growing up poor but also unsettling in some way I couldn't quite define. I had never not worked toward some kind of goal.

"You could focus on your writing full time."

"You mean the very thing I avoid?"

"Seriously, what's up with that? Why did you even get your degree if you didn't want to use it?"

Same reason I did most things—to see if I could. But also, I did want to finish that manuscript on my desktop. It was just hard to stay focused. Hard to balance being out in the world living. "Not everyone has your ability to hyper focus."

"Come on. How many more people have to tell you you're talented? Go for it. These businesses are creative but you've got more in you. You're distracting yourself." I supposed it was ironic. I'd gone into the restaurant business as a teen-ager not only to survive but to pay for college. I'd stayed in the business to ultimately support my love for reading and writing. "It's something to think about," Jon said. "Especially since you can work remotely."

Soon after that conversation, Jon's project broke ground, and he began to spend three weeks a month travelling. Sometimes I went with him and sometimes I would need to return home early to work. As I would pull up to our empty house, I began to wonder what it was exactly that I *was* trying to prove with these places. It's not as if I was running cancer research centers or saving orcas from captivity.

"Heath, you do what makes you happy. But if I were you, I'd sell them and write and travel with me instead. I mean, we have everything we need."

It was late. My feet ached. And I thought he was right. "Do you really think I could get someone to buy them?"

"In a heartbeat. I bet if you ask around you'd find a bunch of people who would be interested. Probably even people you know. And if not, there's always a broker."

"I guess it wouldn't hurt to put the word out."

In the meantime, I dusted off my manuscript, began working on it, and reached out to my thesis mentor—a famous writer I'll call Lorna—who agreed to discuss pages with me at her New York City apartment.

As we settled in at her kitchen table, she told me about the latest book she was working on about a feminist from the 1800s. Lorna was herself a radical feminist. She'd once told a story in our graduate class about how, in the early 1960s, after getting married like her friends, she'd had a wake-up call when her husband, who'd treated her as an equal before marriage, suddenly started asking her what was for dinner. One day she thought, "Get your own goddamned dinner." She then went on to travel, write, and help shape the feminist thought of the 1970s. I don't think I would be stretching it a bit too far to say that she considered even contemporary marriage a form of slavery for women. So I guess I shouldn't have been surprised at her reaction when she saw my ring.

"I thought you wanted to be a writer!"

I laughed and told her how very much in love we were, and how he was a very special breed. "He's smart, he's..." The one pushing me to write.

She held up her hand to stop me there. If I wanted to talk about pages, fine, otherwise, she had to get back to work.

I drove home, slightly put off, but also understanding her hesitations. Besides being a scholar of feminism, writing about women of the first wave who had fought for our basic rights to own property and vote, she had gotten married during the second wave of feminism, when our reproductive freedom was still at risk, our educational, social, and economic opportunities were still inequitable, and the "nuclear family" was a dirty phrase. We'd since begun a third wave and were on our way to a fourth. But as Peter Gabriel's *In Your Eyes* played on the radio, I jacked it up, tuning out the noise of the Long Island Expressway and shutting off everything I had ever learned or heard about those waves, including that excellent quote by Lorna's contemporary, Gloria Steinem: "A liberated woman is one who has sex before marriage and a job afterward."

It was 2005, and for reasons that seemed to make sense at the time, I was about to do the opposite.

"My children always say they want a bigger house, more vacations, like the rest of their friends. They don't understand they have everything they need in abundance."

- Heather Fox, Merrick, married sixteen years

THE CASTLE

I sold the stores, one by one. After that, the rest went easily. I traded in my Jetta for a new lease under Jon's name. I sold my house. I even exchanged my gold jewelry for a small pile of cash, surrendering over the handful of tasteless bracelets and necklaces, including a diamond-plated "H" that reminded him, and me, I'd had past relationships.

Cringing yet? Wait for it...

This, and the rest of the proceeds, I then deposited into our joint bank account. Jon took the helm of the finance ship, and I willingly let him. He was organized and seemed to enjoy it. I'd always treated writing checks the way I had treated doing laundry, an icky job that reluctantly needed to be done. Jon treated it like a meditation.

I'm going to do some bills meant *I'm going to scroll through our automated payments, make tidy entries onto our Excel spreadsheet, and restore order to the world.*

It was a little bit unsettling to be so free of responsibility—and so entwined financially with another person—since I'd been on my own virtually since I was fourteen; but at the same time, I felt a sense of safety I'd never felt before.

The way I saw it, I'd been alone up until that point in time, relying on myself on my own secluded island to do all the gathering of coconuts and hunting for fish. Now I had a hunter on my team—and enough stockpile of gatherings to last as many winters as I could imagine. Add to that the open schedule I now shared with retirees; it was time to finally focus on higher objectives.

So, did I get to work on writing?

Of course not.

Writing was hard work and editing maybe harder—both way more difficult than starting or running small businesses. And without the balance of the two, I fell into a funk about it.

I'd once read an interview of William Carlos Williams, who was both a poet and a physician. Williams said he could never have become a writer without also having been a physician; that he needed the two worlds to balance his ability to perform well at each job. The public, gregarious task of meeting patients, and the private, solitary—and lonely—life of a writer balanced each other.

That was the other problem. I just didn't *feel* like sitting at home in front of my computer like a child made to stay inside and do her homework, or worse, punished. I wanted to go outside and play, which was challenging considering now there was nowhere to go.

I *needed* distraction.

My spiritual classes were all but out at that point. The final straw came when a hevreh pulled me aside at a Rosh Hashanah dinner and told me I needed to slaughter my own chicken for an upcoming event. Adios Madonna, Sandra Bernhardt, Monica Lewinsky, and Marla Maples.

Volunteering also fell by the wayside. When I'd lived closer, I'd been driving once a week for Meals on Wheels and FISH, but now civilization as I'd known it was forty-five minutes away. And the little village in Oyster Bay, with its one diner, a couple of restaurants, a Carvel, and Billy Joel's motorcycle shop didn't count as real civilization for me.

We talked about getting pregnant; both of us were on board. When I pressed Jon, he admitted that he could live without having to save for more college educations, but he didn't want to deny me, if it was something I wanted, so we started trying.

Which took about ten to twenty minutes every day.

I took yoga classes at a local studio, admiring the musculature of the devoted, skinny young housewives, deep down knowing I could never rise to that level of commitment, as I just didn't care enough about sculpting my body parts.

I made social plans with friends, neighbors, even acquaintances—like one of the yogis. "Who are these people again?" Jon would ask as we headed to a restaurant on a Saturday night. "And why are we meeting them?"

I went to the market a few times a week and planned elaborate dinners. Jon loved eating dinner at home, even though my dishes never seemed quite what he'd romanticized them to be—or maybe what I'd inflated them to be. He never said, "This is horrible," but he would silently pout when, after sitting down to enjoy the organic turkey meatloaf I'd been waxing on about all day, he bit into a dense mass of blandness.

I really didn't have to try so hard. He was fine with takeout Chinese. And if we ate at home, he couldn't have been an easier audience; his palette was like a little boy's, wowed by pasta with peas and butter or grilled chicken salad with bottled dressing. But *I* needed the challenge of trying new recipes, like rustic vegetable pot pie, which could have been registered as a lethal weapon, the dough was so tough; or vegetarian stuffed cabbage that, while tasty, resembled vegetarian goulash. Once, by sheer luck, I produced restaurant quality chicken tikka masala, and he raved about it for weeks. When I made it again, even I had to admit it didn't live up to its predecessor. Foodie cooking was apparently vastly different than simple café food.

I orchestrated weekend excursions with Eddie and Emily—outings to grassy fields and farms. "Remind me again why we're doing this," Eddie asked as the four of us traipsed across the Planting Fields Arboretum, me leading the pack, while Jon, happy to be doing something other seeing a movie or going to the mall and then the Cheesecake Factory, stopped to marvel at every twisted tree trunk or lavender planting, pointing out which plants were and were not indigenous to Long Island.

"We're getting out into the sunshine," I'd say. "Seeing the world. Getting our blood moving."

"Yeah, but why?" Eddie asked. "When we could be home, I don't know…napping?"

"I thought we were going to have lunch," Emily said, "or I wouldn't have agreed to this."

I repainted the dining room and rearranged furniture. Made scrapbooks and organized CD collections. And—perhaps my proudest accomplishment—nursed a feral cat back to life. That day, Jon came home to find me sitting on the driveway, trying to feed a hissing cat a bowl of food. I'd been pulling the trash cans to the curb when the poor creature had limped by with a swollen bite on his head, likely from a raccoon. After some investigative work, I'd found a rescue society to call in antibiotics to a local vet, which I had picked up and mixed into a can of wet food.

"What a dope," Jon said, watching the feline who threatened to bite the hand that had just fed him—though I think now, he might as well have been talking about me.

Jon didn't understand cats. To him, they were untrustworthy mini lions that, if given the chance to grow to fifty times their size, would eat the humans who cared for them. He was a dog person through and through. Dogs at least gave back something, he would say, as he stroked my tabby, who seemed to be playing dead.

He was also not used to the shedding fur that floated atop everything. No matter—I vacuumed away, happy in my new housewife role. Somewhere along the way, I'd read that once married, a woman spends something like seventy percent more time on housework than when she was single; in my case it was more like a one hundred percent surge, but I didn't see that as a problem. Housework gave me something to do.

One day, as I was pulling the dead leaves off the lily plant, Jon walked out of his office and told me he thought we should upgrade since more money was coming than going out. "We can do better," he said. "So, why not?"

"Really? But I like it here." I had finally warmed up the place enough to make it feel like a living space and less the lord's manor.

He became obsessed with *Homes & Estates Magazine*. What did I think of this six-bedroom French provincial on seven acres? How about this five-bedroom carriage home on three acres? I had no idea what we would do with more than the three bedrooms we had, but he was excited, so I got excited: finding our marriage home could be fun and romantic. If I couldn't think of a reason we needed to upgrade, I couldn't think of a reason not to either—especially since house hunting could be my new job.

Around this time, we stopped at the supermarket to pick up vegetables for a garden lasagna I planned to make, and he said, "Isn't this that natural peanut butter you like?"

"What about it?"

"It's on sale. You should stock up." He threw three into the basket.

He was a person who liked to live larger than large, I began to understand, when it came to the big things in life—houses, cars, diamonds, electronics. But with the smaller things, especially commodities, he liked to economize. It was the big things in life that made him feel rich. I'd been used to living modestly with the big things. Having the small things—gourmet food, entertainment, and cheap but plentiful clothes— were what really made me feel like I was "living."

Jon told me we could still have both, as long as we were smart. Why not pay the grocery store $3.68 less for peanut butter, he explained, by buying it now, rather than in two weeks at full price? It was a new and interesting perspective to consider stockpiling my favorite brands. I mean, I couldn't exactly argue against getting more for less, even if it did come with a certain pressure to eat three jars of it before May 2008. I did notice that since I'd moved in, there remained unused, five quarts of BBQ sauce, three cases of instant ramen noodles, and eight packages of hot dogs, but who was counting?

The "right way" was a phrase I began to hear around this time. When he saw me trying to hang a picture on the wall, he went for the tape measure. "Why not do it *the right way?*"

I banged in the nail, *close enough*. When he returned and measured the center of the wall, I saw I'd been off by a whole two inches. *Hmmm.*

Keeping up with perfection also came with pressures though. I'd always kept my house clean and neat, but Jon could make the bed tight enough to win accolades during a military inspection. Not wanting to be accused of being the slob in the relationship, I'd fluff the couch pillows when I got up. Though I did draw the line at toweling off my toothbrush.

One night, as I waited for split pea soup to soften, I overheard Jon talking to Eddie about a summer job Eddie wanted at Key Food supermarket with his buddy. He had turned fifteen and his buddy was working there. I thought it was pretty admirable that he wanted to spend his summer earning money, but Jon was incredulous.

"You're not some schlep, Eddie. You can do better than Key Food. Are you kidding me?"

For some reason, I thought of the poem near Jon's desk and went to read it. Jon had written it for his English class when he was fifteen. In clumsy iambic pentameter, he'd lamented about not having always listened to his father's sage advice, about taking his father for granted. The poem also held a subtext.

The right way. I studied the picture of Jon's father—an

intellectual, a doctor, a man of tough love, a man who likely had been implacable. A man Jon had tried to please anyway.

Eddie resisted Jon, sore not only because he wanted to work at Key Food, but because he resented Jon's disapproval of his friend, who'd already accepted the summer position. Eddie had a sort of Robin Hood way about him, defending the underdog.

"But why would you waste your summer slacking off at a grocery store when you could be doing something productive for your college resume? Something that will give you a leg up?"

"Because it's not always about the resume, Dad."

"Do what you want, Eddie. But don't ask for my seal of approval, because you know how I feel."

With Emily it was more about protection. "Careful of that rock. Don't wave the fork around your eye while you're talking."

They'd started to come to me to "get through" to Jon. "You just don't understand how he can be," they would say. I understood he could be demanding, but I thought it was incredible they had such an invested father.

"Well, you know your dad is like that because he loves you, right? He would do anything for you. He just wants you to do your best."

"But can't you just talk to him? He listens to you."

To appease them, I would talk to Jon, playing the role of buffer. Perhaps he could soften his delivery when talking to the kids? "Okay," Jon said. "So what should I have said? Eddie, *please* don't be a loser this summer?"

Eddie took a job at his school's computer room that summer—earlier in the year, he'd not-so-accidentally hacked into the school's grading system, and, on Jon's recommendation, he confessed his crime, then asked for a job, which they offered on the condition he write code to better their security. And Emily was careful to hold the fork away from her eye.

In the end, they were kind of on their own with him no matter how I defended them. They wanted his approval.

I understood why.

"So I was thinking," I said, one Sunday afternoon as we drove through Oyster Bay Cove, seeking For Sale signs. "Whatever house we choose, I would really like to make it somewhat of a farmhouse. Maybe old floors, mixed with modern features? Just nothing too... *fancy*."

"That sounds awesome. I'll leave the decorating to you. I love your taste." *Phew!*

I started a design folder, ripping out pictures of windows, shingles, doors, doorknobs, and cabinets, all with a rustic feel that spoke me of the house we would inhabit for the rest of our lives. Jon seemed to love everything I showed him, which is why I grew confused one afternoon, a week following our one year anniversary, when we waltzed into the open house of a six bedroom, 1980s contemporary house, replete with trapezoidal windows, and Jon declared that this was it.

"What?" I laughed. "This is the total opposite of what we talked about."

"Of course we can change the little cosmetics. But look at the big picture."

I looked around and saw sharp angles every which way. A voluminous geometrical puzzle.

"See what I mean?"

"Trying to..."

"Look at that." He motioned to the backyard beyond the sliding glass doors.

We were in the woods of a town called Locust Valley on a property with four acres of sloping grass and scrub. I saw lots of weed pulling and mowing.

"You have to admit it's an incredible spot," Jon said.

"It is...unique." I slid the door open and stepped outside, trying to absorb his vision and appreciate his ten-years-older (and hopefully wiser) experience. I'd bought two small houses in my lifetime and kept money in the bank. He'd been more adventurous over the years, with interest only payments, whatever that meant; it was the kind of stuff late-night infomercials were about. I could never wrap my head around the concept, nor did I want to.

We went home and he waxed on about potential plans. I'd never seen him so excited, so I agreed to get the house.

I hesitated once, a week before we signed on the dotted line, as I looked over the architect's initial sketch.

"Do you really think this can be done?" I whispered to Jon, when the question I should have been asking was: *should* we do this?

There was, of course, the money—numbers that scared me to see on paper. There was also the space—the sheer amount of it. Something about two people living in all that square footage, with all that land, rubbed *all* the people I'd been the wrong way. This would be our home, a representation of who we were, and clearly, we wouldn't be proponents of Al Gore's "reduce your carbon footprint campaign."

One afternoon, I showed the cabinetmaker to the den, where we wanted to install the built-in bookcases and entertainment center. As I turned to leave him to his measurements, he tugged my sleeve. "Before you leave—how do I get out of here?" Feeling ashamed, I gave him a quick tour back to the front door.

It took close to a year for the house to be completed. And when construction was finished, there stood a beautiful transitional farmhouse. I climbed the stairs leading up from the garage—my belly round and large—our twenty-minute sessions had finally paid off; I was nine months pregnant.

I walked through the oversized kitchen, with its granite countertops and Viking stove, and up the front staircase, running my hands along the oak railings and balustrades, the newel posts—terms I'd never known before. I continued across the balcony overlooking the living room with its fifteen-foot-high ceilings, architectural eyebrow, and bulls-eye windows installed to catch the southern sun and splay it across the walls. I roamed down the five-foot-wide hallway with its thick flat white moldings and paneled wainscoting on the lower halves of the walls. I moved in and out of the bedrooms, deciding on the smallest coziest one for the nursery, closest to the master suite with his and her closets and en suite. I continued down another set of steps that led to the den and more bedrooms and bathrooms, wondering what to do with the rest of this space and feeling a bit incredulous. *We were going to live here?*

And yet, I had to hand it to Jon; it *was* visionary. Yes, I'd picked out paint colors, earthy sages and creams and golds, and chosen oil rubbed bronze hardware for the doors and hinges, wide planked wood floors, nickel plated faucets, rustic sinks, a claw-foot soaking tub, fieldstone facade for the fireplaces, and taupe cedar shingles for the exterior. But changing those rooflines and fixing the circulation? Leveling dirt in the backyard to address sloping issues? Choosing forced-hot-air powered by an oil burner that looked like a jet engine? Actually that was the one mistake we would learn that first winter when the first heating bill arrived—going with the contractor's recommendation for oil when the house was equipped for gas.

Still, I hadn't seen what he'd seen, and I'd secretly second and third guessed our decision—especially when he would travel, and I would be left, in the dead of winter, to check in with the contractor, who was naturally always behind schedule and over budget. I would stand there, blowing steam into the cold air, observing the wall-less and roofless structure, and wonder why we'd chosen to create this chaos and stress, especially when I'd return to our warm, cozy cottage in the woods we rented during this renovation, knowing that those two-rooms were all we really needed, so long as we had a bed, refrigerator, couch, television, clothes, and my cats—the indoor ones (I'd found a local horse farm to take in Dopey).

Jon hated the rental cottage and couldn't wait to leave, though in fairness, he did bump his head daily on the slanted bedroom ceiling. He was excited to pursue larger and better and puzzled over why I would even question it. This was part of the American dream, he told me. It was what people strove for, why they worked hard—to live well and enjoy.

It wasn't a terrible argument.

I moved the throne into his office, as well as the more sumptuous pieces I'd unpacked, deciding if he couldn't part with them, he could house them in his man cave. So, onto the shelves went the tabletop marble bull and glass figurines to compliment his college degrees and complete what looked like a formal library with its floor to ceiling walnut-stained walls, matching desk, and stone fireplace.

The rest of the house, I decorated as unassumingly as possible. Plants and throws, bowls of apples, candles, beat up wooden signs in the kitchen that said things like Rise & Shine Farms.

Still, it was difficult to find the courage to ask anyone over. I'd once been judged for my shoddy off-brand sneakers and subterranean squalor apartment. Now I—more hyper-aware than ever that people were starving and homeless—was judging myself for having a mahogany wood porch.

But I gave it a shot, inviting over a couple we'd met in a Lamaze-type class; she ran a gift basket company, he was in finance. Jon gave them a tour, basking in their compliments, while I spent much of the evening telling them stories about the childhood I had spent living in and out of that basement apartment. "I can't even believe how silly you're being," Jon said, closing the door behind our guests. "No one else is apologetic about living in a big house."

That was part of the problem. I didn't know anyone else who lived in big houses—although that would change as I began to make friends in the neighborhood. I don't think even Jon had a basic understanding of the town we'd moved into. A hop, skip, and a jump away from the *Great Gatsby* world, and where the 1986 movie *The Money Pit* had partially been filmed, the town had a reputation for lockjaw—so I learned one night after joining some women at a sushi-American bistro restaurant with a terrible concept but a good sense of humor.

"Locust Valley Lockjaw Roll?" I read aloud from the menu. "Trust Fund Baby Roll?"

The women I was with, not trust fund babies themselves, but apparently "Townies," like me—people who had transplanted here and were not originally from the blue blood money that could be traced back to early royalty in England—explained that I had arrived in "mini-London" where jaws were held tightly as people spoke.

According to them, the more English the vibe in town, with its antique shops and expensive couture boutiques selling seersucker and other items that seemed straight out of J. Crew advertisements, the happier the Lockjaw crowd was.

So why had these Townies moved here and stayed? The school system, they all agreed, was excellent. And not all the Bunnies, Missies, and Mollies of the area were stereotypically snobbish and peevish. Some were actually very philanthropic.

"Are you telling me there are actually people in this town named Bunny and Missy?" I asked.

"My mother-in-law is Barbie," a tall blonde woman told me.

"But aren't you a Townie?"

"Yeah, it was pretty scandalous. They saw me as a blonde bimbo—and still do. Then again, anyone not worth fifty million dollars are losers to them. So screw 'em."

I came home from that dinner and informed Jon. "You

know, having a Jewish last name, we couldn't get into one of the country clubs around here if we tried."

"C'mon."

"I'm not kidding." I told him the stories I'd heard at dinner including the one about a famous Jewish real estate mogul who was denied entry into a country club.

"Well is that something you even want?"

"Definitely not. You?"

"Fuck, no," he said, proud to be antisocial. He had not moved here to cozy up to the neighbors on golf courses, and maybe not even to live out this so-called dream he was trying to sell me, I began to realize, so much as to secure his castle once again in life. It wasn't about social standing or rubbing elbows with successful people; for him it was about pushing himself to see how high he could climb, about proving the impossible to himself and his deceased father. And it was about keeping the annoying people out. That we were atop an isolated hill seemed to suit him perfectly. All that was really lacking for him at that point was a moat.

As for me, I was glad to have made some friends, and I wanted to make more. So I set out exploring the neighborhood, going for walks, taking in the horse farms and white-painted fences, the hills and valleys, the wide expanses of grass and plantings, and the birch, oak, sequoia, fir, and holly trees that somehow reminded me of Northern California—my primal landscape—and the small window of my childhood, pre family-breakdown, when I still felt at home there.

One night, after having gone for such a walk, I rested my head on Jon's chest, feeling safe and sound, and the parallel opened before me: for the first time in my adult life, I felt at home. Outside, the wind ran through the tall canopies. An owl hooted. Other animals squeaked and called. Our garbage men had told us to be sure to lock down our cans, not only because of the raccoons, but also because of the possums and foxes as well.

"Do you hear that?" Jon asked. I lifted my head from his heart and strained to hear. In the distance it sounded as if something was shrieking. The sound neared, and as it did, we realized it was not an exotic animal, but an ambulance.

We laughed at our stupidity, which somehow turned into kissing—and if there was anything hotter than kissing my husband, I didn't know what it was, especially since we had worked out the kinks and become a solid nine and a half.

"Promise me one thing," he said, rubbing my basketball belly.

"What is it?"

"That we will always have sex, every day, until the day we die."

"Absolutely," I said.

And I kept my promise.

For thirty more days.

"Who cares? You have your kids. You can leave now."
- *Anonymous*

PRINCESS JULIA

Dear U—,
Please oh please don't let it hurt too much.
Yours,
Heather

I squeezed Jon's hand. It was the last moment it would ever be just the two of us, and I felt full of gratitude and terror as I hunkered down, letting the pain in, trying to use it as the birthing books had suggested. I squeezed my eyes shut inside my basketball-sized head, and bit down on my sausage lips. For some reason I could see a rollercoaster ride going up and up. She was born on the way down.

"Hello," I crooned to our little pink alien glow worm with wet curls of blonde hair. We named her Julia. She squinted waxy eyelids at me and cried. Then cried more.

It's the most natural connection, those same birthing books said about breastfeeding. Not to this person. I tried every hour on the hour for the next twelve hours, panicked that she wasn't getting enough milk and worried about whether I would be a good enough mother. She squirmed (and maybe ate?) and cried more. Then I cried.

Jon walked in during one of these sessions, and relief flooded me. He had done this before—or at least witnessed it. He must have some clue about how to help this little creature. "You know the guy at your favorite store only eats dirt, right?" He handed me my requested carrot juice. "I asked him how the chicken salad was, and he told me he doesn't eat meat. I asked him how the Caesar salad was, and he told me he doesn't eat dairy…"

"Wait…shhh. I think she's finally asleep."

"Okay." He kissed me on the forehead. "I'll be down the hall."

"What? You can't leave!"

My roommate moaned from behind a divider curtain—my nightmare roommate who invaded my room that morning, left a trail of bloody pads to the bathroom, and wailed to her mother through the night about not getting her baby to latch on either.

"Heath…" he nodded toward the curtain, lowering his voice. "I can't sleep here now." Moaning turned to screaming. "Besides, you're doing great."

"I don't think I am. I need your help."

"You think *I* have the answers?" He laughed, and I saw not only my nerdy engineer, clueless about boobies and milk, but a glimpse of the person he'd been in a previous life, allowing his ex-wife to tend to diapers and bottles solo. It had never been his domain. Mine either!

Three days later, in the back of the SUV, I fumbled with Julia's car seat, trying to decode how the clips worked. I moved slowly, working against the knives in my crotch and cement bricks in my hips, trying not to shatter our glass baby as I maneuvered her tiny body into the car seat. Understanding that this monumental task was now all on me, I had decided over the last few days to embrace it. *Another chance to grow.*

I'd also decided that if there was one thing I was going to get right, it was everything. I wasn't going be a good mother. I was going to be a great mother. I had a daughter, and that rocked my world.

"What's taking so long?" Jon asked through the rearview mirror as he waited for the satisfying click of the seat buckle.

"I can't get her positioned right."

"Well, you're obviously not doing it right."

His tone was wrong, all wrong: protective of our cub, and upset with me. It rattled me. "Would *you* like to try it?"

He came around to the backseat and proceeded to deal with the same blobbery issues, akin to squeezing a bowl of porridge into a rigid mold of plastic and steel.

"It's the seat," he muttered. "They should have made it so it tilts back more. Where's that headrest thing you got? That will probably work."

"Home," I said, as in "naturally." In my thirty-eighth week, I'd gone for a check up to find that my water was leaking, and, having been admitted spontaneously, I hadn't finished packing the advised hospital bag.

"Of course it is," he muttered. And I stood there, blinking, as if a total eclipse had just swept over the land and left me in the dark cold.

What the hell was his problem? I took a deep breath. Clearly, he was as panicked and as scared as me. So I decided to let it go. We drove toward home silently. Now and then, he glanced back. "Is she all right? Should I go slower? Are you watching her?"

She's fine, I wanted to say, but I'm not. *I just had a baby. I need cuddles and encouragement and nurturing and support!* But I kept quiet, feeling ridiculous. I obviously wanted him to care for her safety. I figured he'd relax when we got home.

When we got home, his panic gave way to increased protectiveness of her, and as a by-product, increased criticism for me. "Careful, watch her head...I don't know if you're strapping the diapers right...are you kidding? Organic diapers? You think her ass knows the difference? And what's this? California Baby diaper cream? What's wrong with good old Johnson and Johnson?"

The right way.

"Jon!" I snapped. "Can you *stop talking*?"

That's when he looked at me as though I'd started to morph into someone else too. Which, of course, I had.

If his paternal instincts were somehow overstimulating his micromanaging tendencies, then my maternal instincts were dialing up my intolerance for those tendencies, if not also magnifying my own need to keep everything toxic away from Julia, including ammonia-laden diapers and creams with scary ingredients, whether or not her ass knew the difference.

"You need me to *stop talking*?"

"I need less…direction, okay?" I rocked Julia, swaying back and forth, trying to get her to stop crying. "And she needs peace. Look how upset she is."

"She's upset because she's uncomfortable." He took her from my arms, patted her back, released a belch, and quieted her. Well, point one for him.

To the outsider looking in we were, of course, an average couple dealing with the stress of a new baby, and our less-than-perfect communication was par for the course. But to me, an invisible tectonic shift had occurred, and it shook me to my core. Right when I was most vulnerable and needed that strong sense of family and security—right when I need-ed that sense of home—was the moment I felt most alone, cut off from the warmth of his sun.

It didn't help that I was exhausted and physically trauma-tized, or that he resumed his usual routine of going back to work, while I got up at all hours of the night, and then tried to maneuver through a strange twilight-daylight haze of breastfeeding, laundering white cotton onesies, pumping breast milk, and napping, all while trying to regain a sense of normalcy.

But nothing was normal in that haze—including my sitting in the backseat while Eddie or Emily rode shotgun.

"Well, don't you *want* to be next to Julia, anyway?" Jon would ask as we piled in.

Of course I did. And that was the bummer: I wanted to be skin to skin with our glow worm at all times. I couldn't have stayed away if I tried. At the same time, I resented being usurped from sitting front and center with Jon as much as I resented the inequities baked into this traditional role.

We were two years in, just in time for our wedding anniversary, and also, as anthropologists suggested, for our romance level to fade, or, as scientists suggested, for a marriage of opposites to reveal hardships that a marriage of similars might not face. Remember the shoebox in the garbage? Well, this time it was a diaper box inside the garbage.

"You've got to be kidding me, Heather." Jon stomped on it, folded it, and then reminded me that he still had no problem taking out the trash. Which was true, if by "no problem" he meant announcing in real time that he was taking out the trash, if not reminding me at every available opportunity for the rest of the day that he'd fulfilled that duty.

"Jon, it's just a box."

"A box that takes up the entire garbage bag. Does that make any logical sense? I mean, really."

"You don't have to get so worked up over it."

"You should get *more* worked up over it. You want to save the world. Start with the environment."

My apologies to the environment. I had baby brain. Or maybe I *was* being a lazy jerk not to flatten the box and set it into recycling. But even more pressing to me was why we were seriously taking ten solid minutes to argue about this. Or why our metaphysical love with circles and dots wasn't conquering all. Or why the hell he had to seal the toothpaste so damn tight! And to think I once revered his attention to detail.

"All I did was close it, Heather."

"Look at my tooth, Jon. I think I seriously chipped it trying to twist it open."

And then there was the underwear battle. Jon suggested that since it was just as easy to fold underwear one way as another, why fold it the wrong way, aka my way—folded into two, and then into two again—when instead I could fold his tightie-whities *the right way* (complete with a demonstration) into three, then into two, and then into two again.

"Are you making calzones?" I asked.

He grimaced and stormed out. What had I called these differences between us? Fun chasms?

More to the point, I thought, carrying the laundry basket upstairs, equally mad, and also stubbornly refusing to make Italian pastries out of his briefs, not only because now I resented doing his laundry, but because his three-fold technique was beyond ridiculous, and because he was perfectly capable of micromanaging his own freaking underwear. What the hell had happened between us? And how had it all happened so fast?

Tucking his imperfect undergarments into drawers, I drafted in my head the sequel synopsis to *The Missing Piece Meets the Big O*, which I titled *The Missing Piece Domesticates with the Big O*.

And the elevator pitch went something like this: When the Missing Piece and the Big O hunker down into domestic life together, it doesn't take long to discover that the very things they'd once found endearing that had completed them as a couple, now seemed to most irritate each of them.

Chapter One: *I Refuse to Make Calzones.*

"Without love there is nothing. And sometimes love is not enough."

- H.G., *Glen Cove, married thirty-eight years*

THE GREAT DIVIDE

Was our first year after Julia's birth a total struggle?

Of course not. But we'd definitely stopped staring into each other eyes with heart emojis. I no longer listened, fascinated by his tales of conquest at the office. He no longer asked after my day. I no longer asked for his opinions on which appetizer I should order. Ouch. That one really bothered him.

"I'll take the grilled artichoke," I would say, handing back my menu, his hurt palpable. If there was one thing he disliked ordering at a restaurant, it was artichokes. "So much work for so little food," he'd once described them.

"Why don't you get the fried calamari?" he suggested, hoping for some of mine as usual. "I bet it's delicious."

"Because *I* don't want calamari."

Needless to say, the sex wasn't going great either, plummeting from a scale of ten to all time low of two, if and when it happened. "You awake?" he'd ask, climbing into bed, and I would feign sleeping.

Other days, I'd enter the bedroom to find him asleep (or perhaps playing possum, too). That burned me up. I would seethe inside and curl fetally, the realization like a hot brand on my skin: *He doesn't even care if I'm in this bed!*

Those nights I'd glare at the Klimt print, now hanging in our bedroom, and scoff. Who the hell made Gustav the expert on love, anyway? One night I Googled to find out more about him. He loved women—many of them, in fact. With them, he fathered fourteen children.

And never married.

It made me laugh, but it also made me wonder if our underlying friction had as much to do with our personalities as it did with this legal institution somehow squashing our love and getting the better of us by pigeonholing us into the Matriarchy and the Patriarchy. Even thinking about our roles like that could sap the romantic wind from my sail and explain some negative facts about marriage. Like why the divorce rate is so high, or why the marriage rate is on the decline, or why people gain weight during marriage, or why spouses are always the first suspects in murders. Or was something else to blame for our issues, I wondered, as I glanced from my laptop to the back of his curly head on the pillow beside me, still so much like the figure in the painting.

What if I'd been right initially: that there was no such a thing as a be-all-end-all person, and all those signs and messages had been manufactured in my head?

Or, equally as troubling, what if there were, in fact, *many* kinds of soulmates? I mean, if I thought about it, I'd had best friends, who I could argue were my friend soulmates, and siblings who were sibling soulmates. What if Jon was my marriage—and not necessarily lifelong—soulmate? Or my baby daddy soulmate? Had all those signs and pointers really just led to me having Jules, my daughter soulmate?

Speaking of which, I couldn't totally rule out biology as one root cause for our troubles either. The dopamine surges and the oxytocin that once fixated me on Jon, probably for the procreation of the species, now had me fixated on Jules. They had been released during childbirth, and I swore I could still feel the chemical changes. It wasn't even a question about whether I would give my life for her. I would take any disease for her, crawl through raw sewage for her, kill for her. I closed my laptop and considered the painting again—and the question I'd asked myself from the beginning. Would you still drink the poison for *him?* The honest answer was that I couldn't if I'd wanted to. I had to live for Jules.

And by the sound of his exasperated sigh, because I was still up with the light still on, he clearly wouldn't be drinking it anytime soon for me.

We got a babysitter and, on my suggestion, returned to Starbucks to talk—the same coffee shop in which we had fallen hard for each other. I opened the door, feeling anticipatory, hoping to regain some of the mysticism that had been present during our first meeting. But no images of Jon on horseback in Mexico flashed before me, and the coffee was too bitter. It had been only three years since we'd nestled into that corner table, and yet, it felt like we had traveled through wormholes in time.

He missed being heard, he told me; he missed me listening to him. He was jealous of how giving I was to everyone but him. He hated that I bought things like probiotic granola or flax crackers—what the hell were those things?—or any number of things in our pantry. Why couldn't we have normal food?

I reminded him that he used to indulge my choices, and if not like them, at least tolerate them. Besides, I didn't want Julia eating garbage. Why would he want her to? "But she doesn't eat them. That is the point," he told me. "We spend money on things that we waste."

It was true she loved a food one day and hated it the next, but kids are fickle, I explained. Maybe I should take control of the checkbook, so he wouldn't have to stress over the small stuff. That wouldn't fix the waste, he told me. Besides, he didn't mind dealing with the checkbook. Code for he couldn't give up control of that checkbook if his life depended upon it. Though if I were being honest, I still had no desire to take it over either. I was grateful one of us was still paying attention to our fiscal life.

"You need to lighten up," I told him.

"And you need to get more serious."

"Why do we have to care about every little thing?"

"Why shouldn't we care about the details?"

Eventually, we zoomed to the core of our issues: we both missed being the bomb to each other. We both missed thinking that the other was the bomb. I missed his sunshine beaming down on me. He missed my nurturing orbit around him.

He took my hand in his. "So what do you want to do?"

And just like that—with the smallest gesture of niceness from him, and with the simple touch of his skin against mine—I was able to see him clearly again. He looked vulnerable, earnest, and dejected at the thought we had both been mulling over: *can we get past all this?*

I jumped into his lap and threw my arms around him. "There you are," I said.

"What are you talking about?" But I could tell by his smile he knew exactly what I was talking about. We hadn't seen each other for months—maybe even for the whole year.

"We just need to get back to our magical place," I said, thinking of us in Turks and Caicos, when we'd dunked in the water and the world had disappeared around us.

"I would love to," he said.

And the question loomed. *How?*

He set down his paper cup. "Why don't we just move forward?"

"That's it? That's our whole plan? Just move forward?"

"Well, we can be sensitive to each other's feelings. But what else are we supposed to do?"

Move forward. The more I thought about it, the more I liked it. It sounded simple and easy.

And maybe it would have been if on September 15, 2008, Lehman Brothers hadn't crashed and burned.

If the top five stressors on a marriage were, in no particular order, parenting, work, sex, chores, and money, we, in no particular order, started making our way through the list.

Jon paced the house, shell-shocked that first month, concerned during the next few months, and worried as the year came to a close and he got the news that the Turks and Caicos project was being boarded up until further notice. Lehman Brothers was the financier. "I still can't believe it," he said, shutting off the television. "The government chooses to save AIG but not Lehman?"

"Well, we had a good run," I said. "I enjoyed it."

"What do you mean?"

"This." I waved my hands in circles, gesturing toward the moldings and high-hats in our den. "It was fun while it lasted."

"Heath, we can't sell this house. It's the worst possible time. People aren't buying. And if they are, sellers are losing their shirts."

"Oh...well. I just assumed since we have to start living off savings that we should probably downsize. I mean, can we cover all our bills...what about Eddie's tuition?" He'd just been accepted into the University of Pennsylvania to study computer engineering.

"We'll swing it until I figure something out," he said, looking suddenly very leonine again, as he had on our first date together.

It was a look I'd once wanted to nurture him for, thinking it signaled his desire to travel the plains with a pride. And while that probably had been the case, the married version of this look, if not also the lion expressing it, was slightly different; for Jon had not only absorbed me into the pride but had taken on the entire responsibility as sole hunter.

Whether I liked it or not, the post-Lehman crash would fundamentally change our dynamics.

"I'll let you know when it's time to pull the rip cord," he said, as if reporting on the status of our remaining carcass. "In the meantime, let's just be careful about spending."

I agreed, forgetting for the moment how very different our core values were, but also not yet *fully* understanding that being careful to Jon meant something entirely different to me—which is why I called ABC Home and Carpet and cancelled the order for our new coffee table, a table it had taken me months to agree to. I'd been perfectly happy with the $200 pleather ottoman I'd snagged from the HomeGoods store, which Jon hated for its smallness and inferior quality.

"You didn't have to do that," he said, as we set the table for dinner the next night.

"I thought you didn't want to spend money?"

"I'm talking about all the other stuff."

The hairs rose on the back of my neck. "What other stuff?"

He headed to his office and returned with an envelope— it's blue and white markings spurring the title of Chapter Two to form in my head: *The Dreaded Amex Bill.*

"I thought we weren't going to do this," I said, knowing at the same time that we'd never really resolved anything with our "move forward" routine. And also feeling torn about the uncomfortable shift in our dynamics. Yes, I was happy he was fiscally responsible, *but* not if it was only according to *his* agenda.

"Vitamins.com…Lifeforce Laboratories…" He began listing my offenses. "Rising Tide, Rising Tide, Rising Tide. You know their groceries are twenty percent higher than every other market, right?"

"No, they're not," I said, knowing they probably were. But they were a small store, easy to navigate a baby seat, and they offered the shiny promise of health, and made me fear that if I *didn't* feed my baby their food, I was a terrible person, a truth I'd take to my grave before admitting to Jon.

"Listen," I offered. "Just because we share different values doesn't make yours better. I don't want to nickel and dime our health."

"Heather, but seriously, let me ask you. Do you think your body really knows the difference between an organic strawberry and a conventional one? Really. I'm seriously asking."

"Actually, yes." I sat down at my kitchen desk and uploaded a website. "Here's a medical study that shows that organic fruits and vegetables have more nutritional value than conventional fruits and vegetables—"

"—says the website that sells organic fruits and vegetables." He hovered over my shoulder. "Mercola.com? Gimme a break. Show me a medical study from Harvard and then we'll talk."

Admittedly, even I knew Mercola.com's advice was suspect at times—I mean, I wasn't about to down krill oil just because a guest osteopath said I should. Although I did think about it. But that was beside the point. The point was—even if he *was* right—what happened to open to my way of thinking? Hell, what happened to *liking* my way of thinking?

Also, couldn't he see that *he* was the one ostensibly being "had" by blindly accepting mainstream products? Nabisco and Proctor & Gamble could only hope for more cradle-to-gravers like him who cared not to question the laundry list of ingredients in Wheat Thins, Rice-A-Roni, and Doritos.

"I'm not going to buy *food stuff*," I said, putting my foot down.

"Well, then stop buying all this other garbage. Every day there's something new."

"That's ridiculous," I said, kicking the truth under the desk (a truth exemplified by the glossy white bag from a major bedding and bath retailer, which was filled with soy candles we didn't need, a garlic peeler I would probably never use, an egg poacher I would definitely never use for that fantastical Sunday brunch I would certainly never host, and two sets of new water glasses we couldn't fit into our cabinets if my life depended upon it).

Because here was another truth: retail therapy offered a temporary fix. And I needed *something* to normalize me after Mommy and Me classes and to fill the hole that widened each day that I set out to battle the small inequities of a life

I had voluntarily chosen and accepted. As Germaine Greer once put it succinctly, "The real theater of the sex war is in the domestic hearth."

Yes, I wanted to be the primary caretaker. But some way, somehow, as I happily changed diapers, slow cooked rice cereal, and sang along to "A peanut sat on a railroad track/ His heart was all aflutter," I felt myself losing my grip on the handle of something I couldn't quite place.

Also, to get real, I knew that we weren't in dire straits. Our savings *was* being depleted by the month, and that was scary to see, but even being able to stay in a holding pattern like this was still a problem of the Western world, first world, middle-to-upper-middle-class couple. And he knew it.

At night, we watched the news and heard the sad stories of the tens of thousands of displaced people who had lost their homes because of Lehman's fall. And in the subsequent burst of the housing bubble, there were people who wished they had time to figure something out before pulling their rip cords, if they even had rip cords, and Jon, who at heart was a liberal mush inside, would sigh, stressing for them.

Had he come to me and said, "Heather, for real, it's time." I would have gladly moved back into that little cottage we'd once shared. If push came to shove, I would have happily lived off bananas and peanut butter (fair trade and organic *if* possible). But he had made the choice for our greater good to hold out. Yes, for appreciation and mortgage rate reasons and stuff that still bored me. But also for his own personal best reason.

The right way.

I did notice that he rarely bought small luxuries for himself, fine as he was with his uniform of dark-colored T-shirts, sports jackets, and jeans—one pair in particular that I had to confiscate to wash. But I also noticed that he hadn't stopped buying the bigger luxuries *he* continued to value as important—new speakers for a sound system that didn't need it, an upgrade on an iPhone when the old version was working fine, detailing of his already impeccable Mercedes.

So I did what any self-respecting woman in my position would do when she realized she'd allowed those value differences to go mostly unvoiced and unchecked on her end— which had led Jon to thinking his way *was* the right way. In a passive aggressive fashion, I did what I wanted, ignored his complaints, and, come early evening, too tired to argue about it, I poured myself a glass of Pinot Noir to dull the noise.

But it never worked.

"You're different when you drink," he'd say.

"Me and every other human being."

"No, I mean you're really different. It's like you can't handle the alcohol."

"Please, I've had one glass of wine," I'd say, sounding and feeling out of control from the moment the alcohol touched my lips.

Then, as the anesthetizing beverage kicked in, with dinner baking or sizzling in the background, I'd turn on Alt Nation radio and try to check in with myself by signing petitions to stop the use of beagles in animal laboratories, or Angora rabbits from getting their fur plucked for sweaters, then I'd scour my horoscope for clues to happiness.

"Your lover is on your nerves today..."

Yeah, no kidding!

Those were the days I would walk with Julia in her stroller through the neighborhood for hours, trying to connect with nature and trying to tap into that sense of home (but not pulling either off). Those were days when both my early childhood and the safe and sound feeling I'd had while snuggled up to Jon's chest seemed like distant scenes from the past. Those were the days I'd slow to peer into people's houses, as I'd done in East Meadow—though, by then, most of the enigma had been demystified.

I knew many of my neighbors' familial stories and

struggles. I'd learned of them over coffee and girls' night out dinners where we would order yet more wine, and they would let loose about their own arguments and estrangements, about their own opposing values and ideals, about their own bickering over children, money, and sex. Save for larger mortgages and tax bills, their struggles were identical to my South Shore suburbanite friends who'd subscribed to the program of marriage and family. Women who'd bought into the dream and somehow wound up in a predicament of dependence.

That's when old plot lines would surface in my head from trashy novels I'd once read as a teenager—melodramatic stories of wealthy, worldly people who, for some reason or other, were unhappy in their relationships and circumstances. And I would remember the sixteen-year-old me, the girl who'd scraped together car insurance payments for a rusted five hundred dollar Cordoba that smelled of maple syrup on account of its chronic antifreeze leak, the girl who would think to herself *God, if I had money, I'd never be unhappy.*

But I began to understand those thoughts were the same naïve thinking as the person who balked at the personal success of a celebrity, like Oprah, when she'd lost her weight, a person who thought to themselves, *Well, if I had a personal chef and a trainer day in and day out, I'd lose weight too.*

I'd been penniless, then I'd had some money, and then I'd had some more money. But happiness is in the heart (at least past the earnings of $75,000, the point where money seems to offer no added happiness according to researchers) and so is suffering. They're both relative.

Not too long ago I had dinner with a friend, a single school teacher in her forties, never married, no children, and she sighed, *Oh the pain and anguish*: if only she could figure out a way to do the one thing she'd always wanted to do.

"What is it?" I'd asked, on the edge of my seat, expecting a soulful revelation.

"To go one hundred percent vegan," she'd said, completely serious. "I've tried every which way, but I just can't seem to digest chia seeds."

Okay, that was ridiculous.

And so was my driveling, I consciously decided. I had long since stopped being an underdog in life. As a thirty-eight-year-old white woman who had a nice home and a family, who had nice throw rugs and paintings to sell if push came to shove—dependent or not—what right did I have to sniffle over not feeling loved and adored as I once had? Really now. I had running water, shelter, democratic freedom, basic human rights, *privileges*.

The self-pity sometimes crept in anyway.

I supposed it was a human thing, the fault of pesky DNA inherited from Homo sapiens ancestors who understood that their health and survival depended upon loving and being loved. Those who didn't feel loved strayed from the herd, ate poisonous berries, and died alone.

I didn't want to die alone, but I couldn't figure out how to feel loved again either.

"You go through waves. I lost myself and found myself many times. I just lost myself again now that my kids are grown."

- D.C. Massapequa, married thirty-two years

THE UPRISING

I fell further into the soft folds of motherhood, the thick honey of toddler time, disappearing into Julia's soft, peachy skin and wispy blonde curls, luxuriating in warm sippy cups of almond milk, *The Hungry Caterpillar, Goodnight Moon,* a ladybug lamp that threw illuminated stars onto her pastel pink and green walls at night, mothering blogs, *What to Expect When Your Toddler is...*sixteen months, eighteen months.

She was my sun now, different from the bright yellow of Jon—more like a soft glowing light that became the center of my existence. I got such a kick out of her innocence, over her reach for language. "Key-cat!" was her first word, pointing to our tuxedo cat, and I'd run to Mother Google, my surrogate that was guiding me through this beautiful hazy dream world, and typed: At what age do kids begin speaking?

Jon starting hearing "Dad" from the moment she'd started pointing at random things, talking to us, "Dah! Dah! Dah!" She wanted *him* to share in her discovery of doorknobs and floor crumbs; he was happy to learn. It was not until a year later, while watching a video of her, that I would realize she'd been saying "that" all those times, but I didn't have the heart to tell him.

We were attached at the hip, she and I, almost literally. I needed to see a chiropractor because I walked crookedly; for some reason I could only get comfortable resting her on my right side, and she insisted on being held to see the world from a higher vantage point.

At night, we snuggled in her full-size bed, in her cozy pink womblike room where time barely moved, where a half hour felt like a minute, where I could endlessly watch her obsess over a compact mirror she never tired of opening and closing, growing more joyful with each satisfying click.

Jon would often join us after his shower, throwing us off kilter as he weighted down the edge of the bed while wearing his red T-shirt, I called the Santa shirt, and a pair of flannel pajamas. His day had been spent at his desk, as it had for the last year, trying to recapitalize the Turks and Caicos project, and to negotiate other deals that had yet to close. At around 6:00 p.m., he'd surrendered to the gym to bench weights and burn off stress on the Stairmaster.

I felt for him. His face was changing. His brows furrowed more. He looked older, yes—he was pushing fifty—but tension had become part of his expression. Always within reach was that one special deal. Then the closing month would arrive, the deal would fall through, and a new deal would inspire hope; all as we whittled through the meat of savings and cut into retirement bones.

We had long since used the money I'd thrown into our pot, which added to my dependence issue and reminded me of a kernel of wisdom from Kabballah class I wish I'd heeded: *Don't give away a cow that provides milk.*

"Still no rip cord?" I'd asked once or twice, regretting each time, as Jon would seize my concern over our finances as an opportunity to gripe about new coffee mugs or yet another new set of throw pillows.

"Oh, my god, Heather, how many freaking pillows do we need?" he exclaimed one night as we undid the bed for sleep.

The answer, of course, if you're fulfilled and happy, is zero. And if not? The answer is eight for a California King to be styled for optimum romance and coziness. Three large in the back, followed by two medium in front of those, accented by three small (or two small and one button pillow).

But I couldn't come clean about my desire to manifest more love through bedding, in part, because I didn't know that's what I was doing. I also couldn't yet articulate how powerless I had started to feel and how viscous the cycle of doing nothing about it had become. So instead, I edged away and snuggled into the pink, watching as the light from the small crystal chandelier in the center of the ceiling cast multicolored lights onto Julia's cheeks, understanding *this* was what mattered.

Because, really, who even cared about those freaking pillows or the lonely ache inside that made me buy them? And if I was being honest, who even cared about this house and keeping it afloat, when all I really wanted was to go back to that feeling I'd had in Jon's arms, or in our little cottage, or on the beach, or somewhere back in Mexico, circa 1500s (only now with the *three* of us).

Jon settled in and buried his face in Julia's arm. Watching this, I wondered if deep down, he too wanted it but didn't know how to get it from me either.

Jules turned two. I enrolled her in a preschool down the block, and, while I missed her, I was also happy to finally have three guilt-free hours to myself. I would drive ten minutes to the parking lot of the local beach, a small sliver of rocky sand that curved around the Long Island Sound and offered a distant and nebulous gray view of Connecticut that looked almost like a watermark against the horizon. There, I would sit in my car and write—ideas for stories, essays, and an occasional Dear Universe letter.

Can you help us reconnect?

My mind swirled in a dreamy haze, and yet, somehow, I found an ending to my manuscript, which I'd needed to become a mother in order to write.

"Where are you?" Jon would call. "Why not do that here?"

How could I explain that being home made me lose concentration and made me get back to "living"? Staying on the beach, I could escape.

A time for living and a time for writing.

Also, I didn't know how to deal with what I eventually iden-
tified as jealousy. It was not just Jon's devotion to Julia when
she wanted him to read her books at night, or to Eddie, when
he called from San Francisco and relayed tales and adventures from a computer start-up he was working for in Silicon
Valley, or to Emily, when she called to talk about her heavy
course load at the University of Pennsylvania where she also
continued their family legacy as an architecture student. It
was his devotion to *everyone* else—his work associates; Henry
the landscaper; Paco the mailman. Everyone seemed to get
a smile and the benefit of the doubt. Then Jon would close
the front door, mosey into the kitchen where I would be
working at my desk, and ask me in an exasperated voice why
I simply refused to shut the pantry door. "I'm always closing
it. You're always leaving it open."

The right way.

"Do we need to hide our canned goods from the world?"

"There's no need to see them."

"Jon, do you hear yourself right now?"

"Do you hear *yourself?*"

But I couldn't. I was too busy drumming up a title for
Chapter Three: *Can You Believe They Keep Potato Chips Next to
Their Soup?*

One morning, I decided to break through our barriers with
sheer force. There was no reason we couldn't put the nonsense aside and consciously decide to see each other lovingly.
Right? To aid the cause, I dug through my lingerie drawer
and pulled out an outfit I hadn't worn since our honeymoon
phase. Sucking up my insecurities about my post-baby body
and my inflamed skin, I reminded myself of Jon's eyesight
problems and slipped on the black lacey number, replete with
a piece of satin dental floss. Over this, I put on my terrycloth
robe and headed to his office.

He was on the phone, seated at his desk, when I walked in, and he held up his index finger as if to say one minute. I waited—looked through his yearbook photos, re-read the poem to his father, and pulled some stray threads from the leather underside of the throne seat, which had started to sag.

Finally, he hung up, and I dropped the robe. "Hey." He smiled and came around the desk. The phone rang.

"You can't answer that," I said.

It felt good: physical and rough, like a collision of our separate trajectories. But somehow it ended with us still far away and disconnected from one another.

The phone rang again. "Sorry, I gotta take this..."

Another night, he tried. "Come here and give me a kiss goodnight," he said from his pillow.

"You come here."

"Let's meet in the middle."

But why did I have to meet in the middle when I had last come to him? Couldn't he lean a little closer to *me*? I leaned, ever so slightly.

"What's your problem?" he asked.

"What's *your* problem?"

We both tried one night and arranged for a babysitter so we could have a date night. As we pulled into the parking lot of a Greek restaurant, I extracted a joint from my purse.

"Compliments of your father-in-law," I said, omitting my father's advice that had accompanied it: "You two just need to loosen up a little."

Neither of us were pot smokers per se. Once a year at a party if someone lit up, I might take a hit. Jon might, too, but he didn't actively seek it out either. But desperate times called for desperate measures, and by the time we reached the valet, we were giggling inside a cloud of smoke.

Then I realized our dilemma. "Jon! This car reeks. They're going to think we're pothead losers."

"You think I give a shit what the valet thinks? Fuck *him*!"

I almost lost my pelvic floor, I was laughing so hard; and you know what? Fuck him was right. We had a marriage to save here! I opened my door and stepped out into a scene reminiscent of a Cheech and Chong movie.

"Good evening," the valet said.

"Evening," I giggled.

"Come on, you lightweight," Jon grabbed my arm. We waltzed inside, ordered everything on the menu, and fed each other with our hands.

"Why do we ever fight?" I asked, laying my head on his broad chest that night.

"I honestly don't know," he said.

But my father's marital tool for reconnection had its drawbacks. The next weekend we went for Italian, and halfway through dinner, as paranoia crept in, I suddenly remembered why I'd stopped smoking pot in high school.

"I think everyone knows we're stoned," I said, my eyes darting around.

"I doubt it. But my head is freaking killing me."

Our meals arrived, and instead of Jon making hot passionate love to me that night, he made it to his eggplant parmesan. Never in a million years would I believe that I could be jealous of breadcrumbs and tomato sauce.

By Monday morning we were back on our separate paths.

Around this time, I remembered a line from the movie *A Civil Action* when Robert Duvall's character comments how in marriage there are good and bad years. I also considered my friend's observations: "You've only been married for five years? Your marriage is so young!"

Maybe if we just got over this bad hump, or this infantile stage, we could reset to two people who looked at each other's opposite value systems and characteristics as a positive thing again. *But what if this is the new norm?* the devil on my shoulder whispered to me one afternoon as I closed my laptop and headed to the preschool. What if Jon would forever see me as THE PROBLEM? *If only Heather would close the pantry door.*

He'll change, the angel said, appearing on my other shoulder. *Once he starts earning again, he will feel better, and he will change toward you. And then you will change toward him. And then you will both reconnect.*

No he won't, said the devil. *Because the real issue is that he doesn't respect you anymore.* A chill blew in. Had that become our fundamental problem? *Yes, he does. Of course he does.* The angel waved the devil away. *She asked him. Didn't you ask him, Heather?* I had. The night of a local house party, after he'd made that strange comment.

A power couple had hosted. She was a newscaster. He was in finance. They had four kids. He never took his eyes off her at the party, never took his hand off the small of her back; he laughed at all of her jokes, fetched her food, refilled her drinks.

"Well, when you make that kind of money, I'll rub your shoulders for you and you can boss me around," Jon joked as we drove home.

But I didn't find it funny. "Wow, Jon. So are you admitting that you have some kind of problem with me, because I don't earn money right now?"

He sensed the trap. "Of course not. Don't be ridiculous."

But in my mind, understanding dawned. It didn't matter that mushy-centered, liberal Jon was for women's rights. It didn't matter that we both had temporarily agreed to these roles as collectively the best thing for Julia and for the three of us. If I couldn't help falling into the trappings of stay-at-home mom, however unwittingly, maybe he couldn't help falling into those of the household provider. A patriarch who equated working outside the home and earning money with power.

And yet, I didn't entirely blame him for thinking that way:

for wasn't I losing a grip on my own sense of power that had come from earning and operating independently?

Heather, you're the mother of his child. The angel continued the Mommy War on my shoulders as I sat in front of the preschool. *I am the voice of truth and I say that women—that homemakers—don't need paying jobs to gain respect,* the angel continued. *Besides, you're doing the most important job in the world.* An argument I'd heard somewhere before...where was it?

Ah, yes: from every stay-at-home mother I knew, and maybe too, from the argument-at-large touted by seventy-five percent of the ten million American stay-at-home mothers who believed it, and roughly sixty percent of the rest of Americans who also believed it. And perhaps, even before now, I'd heard the seedlings of this argument for "domestic feminism" pioneered by Charlotte Elizabeth in early Victorian times, when she'd advocated for working women to be *able* to stay home because she believed they were needed there for their moral superiority to help uplift the household.

Progressive for those times, the devil on my shoulder balked. *But it's now 2010, my dear.* True. Which was perhaps why another argument by some radical feminists—that it should in fact be illegal for women to stay home for extended periods—also had some merit, as the stay-at-home role not only reinforced a patriarchal view but stifled women's collective ability to progress.

And yet, deep down, arguments and respect aside—even my own sense of dependence and insecurities aside—motherless-former-foster-child me knew at that moment in time, I didn't want it any other way.

And that, too, was the ultimate quandary.

As Julia went into the three's program, then the four's, she needed me, and I wanted to be there for her, to make her peanut butter sandwiches in the shape of bunny rabbits and hearts, and to take her on play dates. That was the newest activity, getting her together with a kid her age so they could enjoy ten minutes of play and then argue over who had the toy first; or better, sit side by side doing independent activities and ignoring each other.

I would sit on a couch having coffee with different moms in the same predicament as me: smart, educated women who naturally favored all the feminist movements and policies—past and present—enacted to secure women's equal rights economically, politically, personally, and socially, but who had, for their own personal reasons, given up working to stay at home. These were women who I would later learn might be called new "traditionalists" or, as I liked to think of us, new domestic feminists.

In a comradery of validation, we would tell each other that despite the drawbacks, it was still the right choice for us.

Because even as we resisted it, it still *was*.

Then before I knew it, those soft, lumbering days in which noon rolled into two and then four came to a close. That summer I painted Julia's room a deep, muted purple. A few weeks later, the kindergarten bus pulled up and took her for a six-hour day. And, in the way it happens, I met a stranger.

It was a Thursday morning, and I was bending down to pick up a stray toy when I caught a glimpse of a figure in the living room mirror. Someone else was in my house, and she was...cleaning up after my daughter?

Holy shit. She was me.

And she was weak and soft looking. At forty-one years of age, her once straight posture had misaligned. Her cheekbones and jawline had filled in with soft tissue. Her once quasi-toned flesh had atrophied and now spilled over her jeans. Worse, she looked dull. Her pale skin tinged gray in places. And those angry red dime-sized dots? They had become more like continents, trying to accrete and overthrow all remaining good skin, attacking the entire torso, elbows, knees, thighs, arms, and back. Even my dermatologist had become concerned, advising me to consider biological drugs, side effects be damned.

I moved closer to the mirror, searching for a glimpse of the fearless woman who had stood on the beach in San Diego and dreamed of living bi-coastally, or the marginalized girl with a superiority complex who, just six years earlier, had considered life to be one continuous adventure, or the newlywed who had yearned to take on a traditional life.

I moved closer still and pressed my nose to the glass, something I used to do when I was twelve. I'm not sure what made me initially look so deeply into my eyes that one day after an afternoon of ice-cream truck chasing and bike riding, but I had, and it had been a wild experience as, gazing deeply into my own eyes, almost staring past them, I'd let my focus blur, and literally felt my soul staring back at me. *Well, hello there, Heather.*

Now, a set of glassed-over eyeballs mocked me in hollow silence. I was nowhere, if not also going crazy. Had I fallen *too far* down the wormhole of domesticity? Or let *too much* time pass? If I was being honest, I didn't know how women did more than I was doing—how that woman at the party did it, the one with the four kids and doting husband—let alone how single working mothers were pulling off running their homes and...*anything* else.

Maybe those women did deserve more respect than an exhausted, totally ambitionless me—unless reading recipes for t ofu meatballs I would likely not even make or curling up on the couch and mindlessly watching *Millionaire Matchmaker,* counted as ambitions.

I looked at my reflection. My outsides mirrored my insides. The last of my sharp edges had rounded into soft blurs. Thinking positive, setting my sights on something, and following through all seemed like impossible feats.

And yet, I knew I needed to try. Was it really fair of me to expect my husband to look at me adoringly, when I felt like a lump of coal?

I perused Monster.com., talking myself into the idea of starting with a small part-time job. If I didn't subscribe wholly to the Victorian idea that the woman's place should be in the home, I also didn't fully subscribe to the have-it-all working supermom of the late twentieth century either.

But what could I do? I wondered, running into the first brick wall limitation of stay-at-home life. Whatever it was, it would likely have to be entry level again. While we moms voluntarily took breaks of two, five, and ten years, these domestic slumbers were setting us back. Brick wall number two was that this part-time job had to take place within the limited hours of 10:00 a.m. and 2:00 p.m. I considered trying editorial work, but anything decent in publishing would be in the city, full time. I thought of teaching, but I had tried that in my twenties and, long story short, found it to be the single hardest job on the planet. Freelancing wouldn't get me out of the house.

I shut down the computer. Then opened it again.

Whatever it was it didn't matter, I decided, so long as it led to me sharpening myself and angling off some of the roundness and softness in body and brain.

Not to mention, it wouldn't hurt to have access to my own money again. I don't know why it took six years of marriage to remember what I'd intuitively known pre-marriage—that, regardless of whether a woman decides to be the primary caretaker, she needs to create a private fund. Ideally the fund should hold enough for her to live on her own and support her child if need be, and *at the very least,* have enough to buy her own small luxuries without anyone bothering her about it. Actually, I do know why. I'd chosen to believe that others' cautionary tales didn't apply to me, including stories and literature from college that had started to resurface in my mind.

One short story, in particular, flooded back one afternoon as I busied myself with touch-up paint in the kitchen.

By Charlotte Perkins Gilman, the story titled "The Yellow Wallpaper," is about an artistic, creative woman living in the late 1800s accused of suffering from "nervous depression" (who incidentally lives with her rational, scientific husband named John). Discouraged from pursuing her passions for fear that she will go crazy, she winds up spending days studying and eventually peeling the yellow wallpaper in a single room, which actually does make her go out of her mind.

I set the paintbrush down.

I needed a way out.

CRUSADES

Mid-morning, fueled by a large cup of organic French roast, I typed into the search engines *managerial* and *executive* and scoured through the ads.

"District manager for Red Mango." *Hmmm.* "Food and Beverage Manager for Hyatt." Interesting. Was I a self-starter who could successfully inspire and manage a team for sixty-five grand a year? Possibly! My phone pinged and I glanced down at my reminders: *Food shopping—need conditioner and toilet paper! Car service due ten-thirty a.m. Girl Scouts Troop Meeting: Iron on badge & your day to bring snacks.*

By lunchtime, I stepped off my high optimistic horse and skimmed the lesser ads. Could I answer phones for a law office? Help dispatch taxi cabs? Work in the customer service department of a Jiffy Lube? Or maybe I wanted to "work for myself and create my own flexible hours." If so, I could become the coffee kiosk manager at the local movie theatre.

I heated up the iron and seared petals onto a blue vest, knowing that none of those jobs were going to impact anything. The phrase "work for myself" did linger though…

Was that possible again? More to the point: did I still have what it took to run, let alone start, a successful small business? I did have desperation going for me. And not just my own.

We lay in bed one night in November. The wind whipped at the windows, kicking on the heat, and I saw Jon cringe by the light of his iPhone. Slomin's Oil Company had just come, and with the arctic blast in the forecasts, something told me they'd be back again very soon. I could tell Jon's head was spinning with doom and gloom. Understandably.

It had been three years since Lehman crashed. The evening news maintained that the world at large had changed forever. The housing market was at an all-time low. Credit was hard to come by. "You okay?" I asked.

"Just thinking what would happen if I can't pull this off," he said in a tone I'd never heard from him. "What if I can't reinvent myself?"

"You can do it," I said, not fully sure how, but also beginning to understand why mothers said things like, "It will all be okay." Because, what was the alternative? Saying, "We're screwed"? That wasn't going to inspire anyone anytime soon.

"It's all going to work out," I continued.

"How?"

"'Tis a mystery," I said, stealing a line from a favorite movie, *Shakespeare in Love*. He didn't get the reference. But by the faint light of the moon, I saw that he wasn't buying into my unfounded optimism anyway.

He stared at the ceiling, fifteen feet above us, likely damning its volume and endless energy suck. I thought about what a group of girlfriends had bemoaned recently at one of our dinners: they claimed Long Island was a uniquely stressful place to raise a family, not only because of the competitive schools, but because of the extremely high property taxes, some of the highest in the nation, from the north shore to the south, the west end to the east.

"We could move to North Carolina and live in a cheap condo on the beach. It could be romantic."

"You wouldn't survive five minutes in the BBQ-rib-eating South, Heather."

"True. But there are some up-and-coming places. Progressive, artsy places, like Asheville."

"*Second* of all, it doesn't solve the problem. What am I going to do in North Carolina? I mean seriously."

"I don't know. Live? What does anyone do in North Carolina? We have our health. That's what matters."

"Heath, please." He threw off the covers, heading, no doubt, to get the Tums to soothe the worries eating at him.

I felt a small flame flicker inside. And yet—*what to do?*

I wished I was capable of more. I wished that I had gone to school for law or dentistry instead of English. What the hell had I been thinking, anyway? Yet another major lesson learned: if a woman chooses to stay home, she should leave on the high note of a solid career or at least build a new skill set while attending to the house. Why hadn't I learned how to build SEO engines for companies? Or design aircraft engines?

He climbed back under the covers and crunched away at the sweet rounds of chalk.

"I'm going to get a job," I said.

"Heath, come on."

"I think I can still do it," I said, trying to psyche myself up.

"I don't have any doubt you can."

"You don't?"

"But does it make sense to get a job that pays…what, twenty dollars an hour, so that we can pay our babysitter fifteen dollars an hour?"

"That's not fair."

"It's reality, Heather."

"And inequity." I got up and headed to the bathroom.

"What does *that* mean?"

"It means I stayed home and screwed myself," I called from the sink. "I screwed us."

"Come on, you know Julia has thrived because you're here for her."

But was that even true? Arguably, there were two schools of thought. One claimed that children benefited emotionally and academically from having a stay-at-home parent; the other insisted that girls, in particular, who had working mothers as role models benefited in the long-term emotionally, and in their own achievements and careers. Both agreed that a child's development was most affected by the happiness level of the parents.

Did that mean parents who looked at each other adoringly?

I rinsed out my mouth, retrieved my laptop, and got back into bed.

Dear Universe,
What can I do?
What should I do?
What does Long Island need?

That week, I loaded my car with DVDs and snacks for Jules and drove around, considering service voids in nearby towns and villages.

I knew a coffeehouse would not do this time around. Although the ones I'd sold were still running, the concept had become passé. At least to me. Sitting around at midnight drinking caffeine had lost its appeal and felt regressive, especially since I could no longer have a cup past 11:00 a.m. without battling insomnia.

"What do you think of putting an organic yogurt store right here?" I asked Julia through the rear-view mirror. She looked up from brushing the blonde mane of her brown plastic horse and scrunched her nose.

"Yeah, you're right. No one needs more dairy in their lives." I drove to the next town. "What do you think of putting a wine bar right there?"

"As long as I can work the cash register," my supportive five-year-old said. "Can I, Mom, can I?" She bounced up and down, blonde curls bobbing, hazel eyes widening.

"When you're fifteen."

"Then forget it."

I called my sister, the other encouraging female in my life, and pitched some of my concepts. She listened openly. Selling my businesses had never sat well with her.

She'd gotten married two years after me and hadn't

dreamed of giving up her hair salon and real estate endeavors. Nor did she apologize about her upkeep habits that could rival any celebrity's and certainly put my shopping trips to shame. Jasmine needed to look good for her clients; taking care of herself was a number one priority. It showed in her French-manicured gel nails, flawless skin, and layers of thick blonde hair, highlighted to perfection. She thought nothing of training with the supermodel Giselles' personal trainer or flying to Switzerland for a week to have her tooth removed by a certified biological dentist, lest the poisonous mercury vapors enter her pristine temple of a body. Yeah, she kind of lost me there, too, but only on the Switzerland thing; while the biological dentistry claims were still a debate in my mind, there were plenty of such dentists in the U.S.

Sometimes, just to tickle myself, I would imagine Jon having Jasmine as a wife, and it would make my day. I would literally chuckle. If he thought organic carrots sautéed in coconut oil was weird—he didn't quite buy my explanation that coconut oil didn't turn rancid under high heat, whereas olive oil did—how would he like all of his food prepared in a Vitamix or dehydrator?

When I thought about Jasmine having Jon as a husband, however, the joke didn't seem as funny.

"I don't know how you put up with it for this long," she said into the receiver as I pulled to the side of the road. She loved Jon and appreciated his sense of humor and charisma, which he always made available for her, but the thought of someone having a single solitary word to say about the purchases she made freaked her out.

"So, yes, I think it's great if you do something."

"Any ideas?"

"Not sure, but don't rush it. And don't panic. I won't let you become that type of person."

"What type of person?" I said.

"Gimme a break." She knew that *I* knew we were talking

about the woman who had completely surrendered. About mom jeans and suppressed dreams. About timidity and maybe even depression—something, I would eventually learn, that stay-at-home mothers report more often over their working peers. It was then I understood, even if the choice is *never* to go back to work, that stay-at-homers—suburbanites, ruralites, and urbanites, alike needed to somehow maintain a lifeline to the outside world.

"Okay," Jasmine said, tossing me a rope one afternoon, a few months after our heart to heart. "I have an idea." The health food store around the corner from her, she explained, was going out of business. "What if we take it over together?"

What was it that Deepak Chopra wrote in that book I had read many moons ago—the one collecting dust on my shelf? *The heart knows the answer.* I closed my eyes, took a deep breath, and asked the question. Instantly, my heart said, *I have no idea!* I decided to consult an expert and stopped into Rising Tide, the place Jon had accused me of single-handedly keeping in business and asked the owner some basic questions about numbers and margins and profitability. Since I was indeed one of his best customers, he was happy to share information: namely that if he had to do it all over again, he wouldn't. The margins were paltry, with a potential for six percent profit, and though he'd somehow built a high volume of sales, he lived anxiously awaiting the day a Whole Foods came into town to ruin his life.

I gave him the numbers the current health food store was doing, and he told me that they were low, so low, that the only shot we might have to be profitable was by quadrupling them.

How hard could that be?

"Let's do it," I told Jasmine, meaning, "I will do it." One thing I'd learned about partnership with my quasi-celeb sister was that she was usually good for half the money and a lot of inspiration, though not so much the hands-on part. But I was okay with that since I was the one who needed to build back my strength.

Jon came with me to see the store, eyeing the cracked and dilapidated sign with pigeons roosting inside of it, the dusty Power Bars on the shelves, and the flickering fluorescent lighting. "How much do you think it will cost?" he asked.

I didn't think we needed much, and Jasmine was good for half. I felt like I was giving a Power Point presentation to him—and myself—as I constructed my argument for better products, real nutrition, a vibrant juice bar, and some of that magic touch I was secretly hoping I could still bring.

"We can have juice-cleansing programs," I continued. "And a healthy deli…" I made up the idea on the fly. "People need fast healthy food…enough of the bygone era of dingy health food stores." The more I talked, the more I started to really warm up to the idea. Forget barren shelves and crusty offerings, where people who worked and shopped looked like they were dying. *Why was that, anyway?*

"Because they are," Jon said.

I waxed over him: "…and couches and comfy seats…and a farmhouse mural and better lighting, and top-notch juice equipment and a wheatgrass press!" Jon winced. "Don't knock it until you try it. Supposedly, one shot of wheatgrass is equivalent to consuming a pound of vegetables," I said, having read the supplier's brochure.

"So people should expect to get diarrhea?"

But it was when I mentioned Jasmine's homemade kombucha idea that he nearly spit out his water.

"Let me get this straight." He wiped at his shirt. "You guys want to put, what is it? 'Live active cultures'—in other words *'bacteria'*—in a homemade drink, let it sit on the counter for days to turn rancid, and hope people don't die?"

Okay, so maybe the kombucha wasn't perfect. But the rest of it sounded pretty good.

"Did you crunch any numbers?" he asked.

We went for lunch at the diner, and I made up numbers, padding what things used to cost. This was the part I always hated, the bummer of math, threatening to zap all creativity.

He tabulated on his phone calculator and looked up. "Heath, seriously. If you and your sister really think this can work, then we can afford a *small* investment. But we can't lose it."

"You can't put that pressure on me."

"Very funny. What did you work out in your business plan?"

"You mean creative vision?" I dug into my wilted iceberg lettuce. "See what I mean? And this was in the healthy corner."

"Please tell me you guys have some idea what it would cost to run the place."

"Of course we do," I said, though we hadn't actually addressed that yet. We did, however, decide on a vegan recipe for the Kale Caesar Salad, and man was it tasty.

Since the store was located on a corner, I named it Organic Corner Health Market & Juice Bar. A logo designer from Etsy created a tree integrated into the lettering, using orange, green and brown. I oversaw the construction team as they gutted the store, polished the terracotta floors, wainscoted the walls, added moldings, framed the chalkboards and mural of a wheat field with a sunny blue sky, changed out the fluorescents to the newest kind research told me most resembled natural sunlight, painted the walls in earth tones, and hung farmhouse pendants.

Jon held out a check toward our half of the investment as I was heading out to meet the awning company. "You're writing all this down somewhere and keeping track?"

"Of course," I said, because eventually I planned to record things. Right then, I had too much to juggle between Julia and running back and forth to the store, not to mention that I needed to be free to plot and plan and dream.

I took it as a positive sign that within weeks, I'd started to feel less tired, even considering that I was waking up in the middle of the night to jot down menu ideas. But I wanted even faster change. I wanted to snap my fingers and undo all that had gone wrong these past few years. I wanted to time travel back to myself—through the soft, delicious pink, and past the mucky criticism and contempt between us—and come out on the other side, the admired and adored savior of our marriage.

The stage was set. As I neared completion of the store, my sister called to tell me that the storefront next to her hair salon had also opened up, and wondered if, while we were building one place, we couldn't build two, and put a juice bar in there as well, seeing as the salon staff were always ordering lunch and needed a healthy choice. She had just given birth to her first child, a daughter, and surprise, surprise, felt depleted and tired in a way she'd never experienced.

On the one hand, I recognized her ploy to supply herself with unlimited and convenient access to fresh juices—just as she'd maneuvered to save that health food store around the corner from her so she could shop. On the other hand, this could be the fast track I was looking for.

"I guess I could see something there…" I said, more daydreaming than envisioning. "Maybe not juices, because of the tight parking, but maybe, kicking the can here, a spa? Or a makeup store? Something to compliment your salon?"

"Can it have a juice bar?" she asked.

"Maybe. If we merged the idea of beauty?"

She got excited. And then I got excited. And off I went. "Let's say we had natural beauty products and services, *and* an organic juice bar? We could call it something like…Inside Out Beauty Bar."

"I can't believe I'm going to say this," Jon said when I hung up the phone and told him about our conversation, "but that actually sounds more interesting. High end luxury cosmetics sounds like a much better way to make money than health food." I was a little shocked. And now completely amped up. *If Mr. Skepticism liked the idea, maybe it was not only good but brilliant?* I started sketching in my notebook and researching beautifying vitamins.

A week later, Jon handed me a second check. "But now we really can't afford to lose this money," he said. But I could tell he'd started to buy into the dream I had and to believe all I was pitching to the both of us—that I could take on some of the financial pressure, work my own hours, and still be there for Jules. I yanked it from his hand, somewhat manically to get to that fast track, and raced to the lawyer's office to sign the second lease. A month later, I came back for another check. And then another. "Heather."

"Jon, I have no choice. We are knee deep in this thing."

The challenge with creating the beauty bar, I'd come to realize, was that it needed to actually be...well, *beautiful.* People weren't going to buy beauty products if the place was shoddily thrown together. Plus Jasmine's salon had been in Bellmore for twenty years and had a large following; we didn't want to disappoint her clientele.

"We're almost done," I said. "We just have to refinance the house so I can open a third store and then I promise, we'll be all set."

"It's not funny, Heather."

"I know it's not," I said, biting my lip to stifle a giggle. Good god, what was wrong with me? Giddiness to be back out in the world creating? Or rebellion—as much against the patriarchy, as to the voices that said "You can't" when I'd opened my first places? Or maybe I was just remembering that life didn't have to be so serious all the time?

When I was a kid and was told to be quiet or to grow up or

to straighten myself out, the first thing I did was crack up and laugh. Sitting at my school desk with my head down, buried into the crook of my inner arm, I would cry and shake from laughing so hard. Maybe my sense of humor was waking up from its dormancy? I took this as a cue from the Universe that I was on the right path.

Jas and I walked through the finished beauty bar together, admiring the juice bar in the far left corner with its huge blackboard, offering menu items like "gorgeous greens" and "red-carpet ready red juice" that emphasized "anti-aging phytonutrients"; the finished spa room displaying gray-washed wooden floors and sleek white modern furniture and shelving; the reclaimed wood counters holding makeup displays; the Hollywood-lit makeup mirrors doubling the space; the crystal chandeliers illuminating chrome-topped perfume bottles and bubblegum pink lip glosses; and the huge wallpaper mural of a mermaid floating in a patchwork sea as she held a basket of robin eggs.

"I *love* it," Jasmine said as she ran her hands over the countertops and tested the various natural and safe cosmetics. "You're really talented at merchandising. And decorating… Though I don't know about these eggs." She studied the mural.

"They symbolize fertility, creativity, and rebirth."

That's when she looked right through me. "Is this store for you or for the customers?"

"I don't know," I said. "Is this juice bar for you or for the customers?"

We drove to Massapequa to see the health food store and walked through the aisles of grocery, admiring the neatly organized rows of goods with their labels facing forward, occasionally graced by a staff pick sign highlighting a certain cereal, bag of chips, box of crackers, bottle of supplements, shampoo, or cleaning product.

We inspected the fresh organic produce in the large case at the front of the store, checked the perishables in the packed freezers and refrigerators. The terracotta floor sparkled. The deli case glistened. The juice bar gleamed. The couches beckoned. "I can't believe this is the same store," she said.

Jon met up with us to take a look. "I'm proud of you," he said. He hugged me tightly and kissed me.

Wow. I really did pull it off, I thought.

We had a soft opening at the health market and rang in a few thousand dollars that first day. A few weeks later, we unveiled the beauty bar to friends and family for a trial run and rang in $1500 within the first forty-five minutes.

I thanked the gods above, mentally plotted a trip to the Bahamas, and called Slomin's Oil Company for a refill.

"Top it off, Slo Mo!" I said to Jon in the kitchen, after hanging up with them and doing a little jig for emphasis.

"You're nuts," he said. But I noticed that for first time in a long time, he seemed to remember liking that trait about me.

By the end of that first week, I expected Jon to continue to kiss the ground I walked on, and maybe he would have, if not for his new worry of becoming Mr. Mom as I spent more and more time away from home, and he spent more time carting Julia from the bus stop to after-school activities.

He needn't have worried, though, about falling into the trappings of being a stay-at-home dad. We would never see that amount of money rung up in a single day, let alone forty-five minutes, again.

"You want to be right or you want to be married?"
 - M.M., Massapequa, married fourteen years

"Without marriage, you always feel that there is an easy way out."
 - L.M., Old Westbury, married seventeen years

VANQUISHED

From the street, I blew Julia a kiss through her school bus window, then scaled the long driveway to head for a hot shower, wishing instead that I could just crawl back into bed.

Me and my ideas.

What an absolute joke to think that tethering myself to two mom-and-pop businesses would be the answer to fixing our marriage and getting back to myself! It had been a year since the stores opened, and we were barely breaking even. And while some part of me knew that I should be thanking the Universe for not letting them tank, I was, well, having issues with the Universe. I mean, I'd followed all the signs and taken action and where had it led? Down the path to Chapter 11 bankruptcy?

Had there been such a thing as Entrepreneur's Anonymous, I would have checked myself in to their rehab center and put on a straitjacket. As it stood, I had no choice but to draw my sword and try to fight the fight. Because what was the alternative? Letting it all go up in flames? The stores. My marriage. The way back to our love. My ability to function as an independent being in the world. I hit the shower.

A half hour later, with my hair sopping wet, I poured myself a to-go coffee and grabbed my keys. There was no time for blow drying anymore, no time to assemble cute tops and leggings and earrings and lip gloss; it was curly-ponytail-sweatshirt-and-jeans time. And still, I was running late.

That we lived so far from the stores was the first issue.

It took fifteen minutes just to clear the woods and was a solid forty-five-minute parkway drive from there. I had told myself, and Jon, of course, that the distance would not be a problem, but it was actually a huge problem. Not only was there the obvious issue of traffic, the commute cut into my ability to actually work, leaving me with just four hours per day to clock in until I had to be back home for Jules.

Not to mention other wear and tear.

"You're going down there *again*?" Jon entered the kitchen.

"I can't *not* go."

"What about your employees? Why can't they deal with things? At least they're getting paid."

Issue number two: no profit. I threw my bag over my shoulder and sipped from my cup, hot and black. I was done with even the luxury of cream. I had to channel my inner warrior now—although, having been unable to fully re-sharpen myself, how much fight did I really have left in me?

"Well, I can't get her at the bus stop," he called.

"I know, Jon."

"I'm serious. I have a conference call at 3:30. I can't drop everything to get her."

"Okay."

I sped down the Seaford Oyster Bay Expressway, blasting The Kings of Leon, trying to psych myself up for the day ahead, and at the same time, trying to reconnect with that fearless entrepreneur in me. I had no idea what the lyrics to "Use Somebody" meant; what I did know was that the fearless entrepreneur in me was MIA as I unspooled in a stream of worry all that had gone wrong to date.

In retrospect, maybe my sister and I should have spent more time on that business plan. Or maybe learning *anything* about retail might have been a smarter move for me and Jasmine, who called me, six months into our endeavors, to tell me the stores were stressing her out, and she was sorry she had no idea how to help, but she needed to attend to her own troubles at the salon, as well as the post-partum depression from which she finally admitted she was suffering.

Meanwhile, the truth was I couldn't even be mad at her about any of it. She had tried to help me out of my funk, however ill-conceived her offer had been, and the least I could do was support her while she went through hers.

"You just have to start from a place of love..." I would coach her about her most adorable, rambunctious, curly-haired, six-month-old.

And so, to boot, I'd been at it for the last six months solo, traveling back and forth, making adjustments, wondering what might be awry, or where we had gone wrong in the first place. Take the beauty bar first. The store was drop-dead gorgeous. Everyone commented on that when they walked in. Then they would browse, ask a question or two, and usually walk out.

I thumbed through books about the art of retail; clearly, retail was an art form and also an apprenticeship I should have taken up. Maybe I was decent at merchandising, but buying was another story. I'd learned that fact a week earlier from a very successful shop owner in the "mini-London" of Locust Valley, as she explained the three no-no's she'd learned from twenty years in the business: no clocks, nothing with birds on it, and definitely nothing yellow.

What was the logic?

"There is no logic. Yellow never sells," she'd said matter-of-factly, and I'd just stood there, absorbing that absolute truth in her beautiful little yellow-free store, wishing I had met this Dalai Lama earlier, as, of course, one of my first purchases, which would never sell, was a display of Jessica Cushman pocketbooks with yellow stars. My second "never sell" was a jewelry line with a bird motif; my third was an oversized clock, which, while not for sale, loomed over the cash register mockingly. Other items that I'd bought included an exorbitant amount of makeup and facial cream lines. Were there rules about skin and makeup I could have also learned earlier? Yes. Don't buy indie brands. Unless one is a Sephora and can afford to buy in at $100,000 for top-selling lines that people know and seek out, lines like Laura Mercier or Nars, one is probably not going to have a lot of success with names like Rain Cosmetics.

"Oh, this is the line used at the Miss America Pageant," I'd say, offering the shiny sky-blue compact to a woman with a Michael Kors bag draped over her arm and Gucci sunglasses on her head. Needless to say, she wasn't interested, despite the now seventy-percent discount. It got to the point that the one sale I finally scored made me suspicious that I was being punked.

"Do you carry Rain Cosmetics?" a young female voice had asked through the phone receiver. "I need the Vegas eye shadow trio."

She *needed* it? This I had to see. I called Jon to see if he could get Jules from the bus stop, fibbing to him that I had a potential sale that might be worth it.

"This is getting ridiculous, Heather."

You're telling me!

She walked in later in the day: young, beautiful, natural long hair. "Do you live around here?" I asked, trying to get a read and hoping that there existed some nearby secret cult following for this line that had set the store back three thousand dollars.

"Oh, no, my parents do. I'm getting ready for a pageant show on the west coast and the rule is we have to use Rain. I found you on their website as a retailer."

I rang her up. "With the discount, it's $6.38," I said.

"Awesome that it's on sale," she said. "Thank you."

"My pleasure." I handed her the bag, noting that we only needed to sell $2,993.62 more to break even.

I decided I could make a choice: cry about this new life I'd carved out for myself as a shop girl or laugh about it. I cried about it. Then I walked next door to find Jasmine holed away in her office—taking a break from her packed schedule. She was eating kale chips and grilled salmon and reading *What to Expect in The First Year*. I snagged some of her chips and caught her up on the newest development.

"Crazy," she said. "Meanwhile, the natural products aren't selling much either, huh?"

Natural was definitely not selling, nor were the cruelty-free products, labeled with the little bunny I had worked so hard to ensure was on everything. Maybe women liked to pretend they wanted cosmetically safe products or to save animals' hides, but what they really wanted, I'd come to understand, was efficacy—products to smooth their skin and thicken their lashes—regardless of the ingredients or process required to get them. It was a realization too late, as we were out of funds and stuck with what we had.

"And the juice bar?" she asked.

"You mean besides the fact that women are confused about why there are carrots on a counter two feet from a mascara display?"

"But I'm surprised no one wants fresh juices."

"I don't see you ordering them lately."

"Paleo," she said by way of explanation, revealing her latest diet. And I had to laugh.

And then she laughed. And then the two of us bent over, hysterically. And then my alarm on my phone rang, and I said goodbye and headed off to face the next dragon—the health market—as well as my own demons that had begun to surface and roar in my ear. *You don't have what it takes anymore.*

I pulled up to Organic Corner and parked beneath the orange and green awning, thankful that this store, while far from my house, was only ten minutes from the beauty bar, and that by the grace of chance, or maybe luck, was at least doing slightly better than break-even.

Slightly, of course, being the operative word.

Groceries were the big issue at hand there. Based on the previous owner's listing of categories that had sold well, I'd designed the store around them: x amount of feet for cereal, x amount for canned goods…but it soon became clear that no one wanted x amount of feet of anything. Whether because mainstream grocers now stocked most of what we sold or because people could buy them online, we found ourselves, month after month, filling shopping carts with expired foods, dropping them into the dumpster, and watching the shelves get leaner and leaner.

The juice bar was doing well, however, and keeping the store afloat. A good number of people had embraced it, and while they might not agree with all of our Facebook postings like "juice is the new coffee," and "kale is the new beef," and "probiotics is the new wine," and "quinoa is the new bread," many of them had become regulars, including local hipsters and surprisingly some mainstreamers, like Sy, a sweetheart Italian family man who would kiss the staff hello as if they were cousins and would end up losing eighty pounds through the cleansing program.

I'd started slimming down too—if not from juicing, then from stress, there was at least that bonus—although my skin was doing worse than ever. The patches were downright crimson, and new ones formed daily, like fresh cigar burns that hurt like never before.

I walked in, said my hellos, and set to work reorganizing a barrel of bulk navy beans when my phone vibrated in my back pocket.

"Hey."

"Hey," Jon said through the receiver. "She's home and asking for a snack. And she said you are supposed to take her to get cleats today?"

"Ugh. I forgot about that." I twisted a bag and tied it. "You can't run to Village Sports, right?"

"Heather," he exploded.

"Okay, fine," I said, looking around at all I wanted to do and could not. "They're open till six, anyway."

"I don't think you get it," Jon began, listing all he had to accomplish with work calls over the next hour, how it was fruitless for me to be running to stores that weren't making us money. It all made logical sense. And yet I couldn't stand to listen for one more second. *Little alarms.*

I made my way toward the back office, my skin practically igniting. I walked past the empty shelf space I had filled with baskets, water bottles, fake grass—anything to plug those pockets of emptiness that taunted me, not only about the embarrassing failure of these stores, but also of the end.

Of everything.

We put the house on the market that spring.

Jon couldn't bear to be home when the realtors showed it. And soon enough, I couldn't either.

"I like what they've done with the other rooms, but the kitchen, I don't know, something just isn't right."

Screw you, lady, I'd think, even though I knew she was somewhat right. The kitchen was the only room we'd kept intact from the shell of the house when we'd renovated, as it had been fairly new, and I hadn't known much about designing kitchens. A few years later, the idea to swap out the square floor tile with pine planked floors and paint the cream cabinets a farmhouse black, would come to me, but by then, the design ship had sailed.

But as spring turned to summer and summer turned to fall, I no longer needed to worry about being slighted by critical women. Because people just stopped coming. The realtor told us that the house was priced too high, and Jon didn't want to budge. More talk about appreciation and depreciation and value, which was wasted on me. What did these things matter without laughter, connection, happiness, love, and adoration? *Will you make me the luckiest man in the world and marry me?*

My dermatologist looked me over. His newest most cutting-edge machinery, Extract Laser, coupled with the usual light therapy treatments, were not working. If anything, the laser was making things worse because the skin patches would blister and then ooze and then develop hard, crusty layers that would stab at the new skin forming beneath. I had started to lather myself in coconut oil, bandage up the blisters, and then layer myself in tight tank tops and leggings beneath my outfits to seal in moisture.

"I have to be honest, Heather. This is not good. And it's not going to get better on its own. You really ought to consider a biological. Or at least the Methotrexate."

"You know what," I said, "write it up." At the least, I could not let my skin get the best of me, even though by all appearances, it already had: my arms, legs, torso, and scalp were nearly fully covered in a disease that I could no longer control any more than I could fix our finances or the negative patterns that had become established between Jon and myself.

In the parking lot, I tore open the package, and shook out four small pills. Four small very potent pills. The miniature brochure told me I would have to take these two times a day—indefinitely. And then when I stopped, my skin might go even more haywire. I squinted to read the side effects. *Hair loss, bleeding, blue lips, weakness.* Apparently, I'd also need to get my liver tested regularly. More fine print explained that this was a drug used for organ transplanting. It lowered the immune system so that the body wouldn't fight off a stranger's kidney or liver. And with a lowered immune system I could contract something else horrible, like tuberculosis.

I deposited the pills back into the bottle. *Not yet.*

I needed to be here for Julia for the long haul.

I thought a lot about my munchkin, and I worried. The majority of our parental fights were held in private, but she was a smart kid. She knew exactly what was going on, and her personality was being shaped moment by moment by our relationship. She had morphed from a shy, sweet girl to a loud mini adult in a six-year-old body. She was a big, complex personality who commanded attention and spoke to us as disrespectfully as we spoke to each other.

"You're not listening to me, Dad! How many times do I have to say it?"

"Mom, you're not doing that right. You don't know how to do it right. You never do." It was like looking in a funhouse mirror and hating what I saw.

I began to wonder what Julia would be like if she was exposed to our higher selves more frequently. If, say, she bopped between *two residences* where the people who lived there were well-adjusted individuals? Because this is what I assumed living alone would afford me: a chance to develop my own voice again without being criticized. In this fantasy residence of mine, there would be no one to comment on the food I bought, or the hours I kept, or the way I didn't put caps back onto salad dressing bottles. And I would have no one to complain about either. But were these reasons enough to leave Jon?

"People don't leave marriages that are a six," my friend told me over a glass of wine, regurgitating what her therapist had told her.

As I moved through banal tasks at work and at home, I considered her idea. Sometimes, I would put dinner on the table and the three of us would eat peacefully, and then Jon and I would share the task of putting Julia to bed and then we would watch television in an easy companion mode. Even though nothing had been solved—no epiphanies, no breakthroughs—we would coexist in a peaceful neutrality and afterward, when we kissed each other goodnight, I would register that while it hadn't been one for the record books, it had been pleasant enough. But maybe I could never be a "pleasant enough" kind of girl. Maybe I needed action and adventure and passion. Despite this, or maybe because of it, I agreed with that therapist. I needed a more dramatic reason to justify leaving than just general malaise with heightened moments of fury. I needed some kind of pivotal no turning back moment where Jon went from being less-than-perfect to an ogre who I had to call the police on or get a restraining order against. Then I could look in the mirror at the welt on my cheek and have my Tina Turner moment. *That's it! Enough is enough! Julia, grab your teddy bear—we are outta here!*

But Jon wasn't a total jerk. He didn't cheat on me. He didn't hit me. And although he complained about money, he had provided a great home and lifestyle all these years; he was what Harriet might call a "mensch" to his children; he was smart, and devoted... And yet, he didn't look at me with those beams of sunshine anymore.

Sure, maybe this stripping away of romance, year by year, was the inevitability of marriage—and monogamy. *Seahorses are monogamous; they mate for life,* so the attached card to our wedding gift had read. Actually, that was partially true. *Many* seahorses were monogamous *during single breeding seasons,* I eventually discovered. Monogamy, in fact, was tough for most species. The prairie vole and the hornbill bird were doing best, followed by the black vulture, although it's noted that this creature abandons the nest after the kiddos have grown. The Azara's night monkey seems also in it for the kids. Then there are cases of serial monogamy, as in the Caribbean cleaner goby fish. Was it delusional to think that staying with one person for a lifetime was not only necessary but honorable? But what did the phrase "leave my marriage" even mean? And what would I be leaving? Not just a marriage, and not just a spouse, but a family. And my lack of identity within this family. That was the ultimate problem, wasn't it?

There was no leaving my lost self. No leaving my failures and my skin. Alone, in whatever this new space was that I would create, I would still be me, lost and vanquished with broken skin, and he would still be him, lost and vanquished, tabulating on a calculator. And yet maybe breaking up was the only way we would be pushed to recover ourselves and transform back to who we once were?

I brought him coffee and got back under the covers. What were *his* private thoughts? Had he been wondering what it would be like to swim off into the sea again?

"Hey," he said, in a tone so normal and benign that it shocked me. "Thanks for the coffee."

"You're welcome," I said, feeling suddenly like a well-adjusted, civilized human being. *Maybe things weren't as bad as I'd been thinking.*

"What's up?" I asked.

"Oh, nothing, just laying here thinking about the house."

I studied the crinkle in his forehead. "Are you thinking we should give in and lower the price?"

"I think we should take it off the market."

"What? Why?"

"Think about it. If we hang in there and the market rebounds... He launched into percentages and numbers, and I zoned out, thinking about the way we used to lay in bed together, unable to stop smiling.

He sipped his coffee and set it down, and I realized he had finished his financial monologue.

"I was *also* thinking. Maybe it wouldn't be the worst idea in the world if we went to therapy."

"We don't need therapy, Heather. I need to earn."

"You really think that is the fix-all to everything, don't you?"

"Well, it's not going to be sitting in some halfwit's office with some shitty degree from SUNY Albany telling me how to work on my marriage."

"Jon, I'll make sure their pedigree meets your standards before I make an appointment."

"Heather, I'm not going. I don't have the head for it. I have too much to worry about as is. If you want to go, then go. I don't think that will help."

"What will help, Jon?"

"You have to grow up, Heather. Our relationship isn't always going to perfect—neither am I and neither are you. It's going to be tough sometimes, and you just have to accept that." I shuddered to think about that. Stay at a six and just accept it? Blah!

He went to meetings in Manhattan, challenging his pride to meet with headhunters, but the jobs were beneath him. Mid-level jobs people would kill for. But he just couldn't become a "schlepp."

I bit my tongue and studied him over dinner. "I'm not going to be a cog in somebody's wheel, Heather," he said, twirling up spaghetti—of the white flour variation; he had taken to making his own batch to avoid the lentil spaghetti Julia and I ate. "I don't think I would recover."

"Okay," I said, amazed, but also realizing the deep magnitude of his ego. And yet the truth was I had fallen in love with him for that very ego—the very thing that might end up, in part, being his and our undoing.

"But it's not like you're going to makeup school or something," I said. "You'd be managing a sales team."

He put down his fork and met my gaze. "*Please* tell me you're not still going through with that."

I shrugged, trying for cuteness, but we were way past that.

He blinked and blinked, trying to find the words. But there were none.

If his ego was too big, then mine seemed almost non-existent with my eagerness to...try *anything*. And my free-spirited approach—the very thing *he* had once loved about *me*—was now beyond mind-boggling to him.

In my defense about the makeup school idea, I'd had a few epiphanies about the stores over the past year, while watching the reality show, *Tabatha's Salon Takeover*, in which an expert cosmetologist steps into a failing salon and changes things up to make it profitable.

Light bulb one: I knew nothing about cosmetics—something Tabatha would have reamed me out for. Her biggest pet peeve was non-cosmetologists starting a salon as a business and not out of passion for the trade.

Light bulb two: we had people working for us who quite possibly didn't know anything about makeup either. The twenty-something's my sister had hired, I now knew, would have been better off working in the mall and practicing on passersby instead of on Jasmine's precious clientele, who, frankly, deserved better than to be transformed and contoured for their daughters' bat mitzvahs.

"Think of it as a Hail Mary shot at the end of the game," I said to Jon, throwing my pocketbook over my shoulder and grabbing my keys. *For me, the stores, and maybe even us.*

"You do realize that you have a master's degree," he said.

"Now is not the time to be uppity, Jon."

"Marriage tips? I will start with Xanax."

- J.S., Merrick, married sixteen years

"Alcohol, lies and time apart work like a charm for a good marriage."

- K.F., East Northport, married nineteen years

HAIL MARY

And so it happened that Monday afternoon in February. I parked my car next to the train station in Hicksville, Long Island, and walked into the Sophia Louise School of Makeup Artistry. Or as I would later come to call the place, the bowels of hell.

Should I have been suspicious when "Sai," the voice that had taken my initial inquiry, called to confirm my start date ten times? Probably, but I assumed he was making commission on my application, and I, of all people, didn't really have a problem with people trying to get a leg up. What did annoy me off the bat was that Sai insisted that I show up three hours earlier than the start time of the orientation so that I could "fill out paperwork." Was there really that much?

"There's a lot, unfortunately," Sai assured me. "And it wouldn't be fair if we have to cut into the orientation time for the others."

I parked and approached the building, a two-story structure connected to a pizzeria, where a handful of young women wearing what looked like white scrubs—cosmetology or aesthetician outfits, I assumed—smoked. I cut through the cloud and stepped inside to the foyer, where I was greeted by the incongruous smell of delicious doughy yeast wafting in from next door. I made my way up the carpeted, 80s style staircase, taking in the dirty white walls lined with framed close-up pictures of eyes, brows, and lips—outdated looks that I hoped were not a harbinger of what was to come.

I passed more women in scrubs, some bending over sinks and washing...were those mannequin heads? Others were blow drying the mannequin heads. I got a quick flash of the Barbie head that Julia had in her room and the fake curling iron that went with it and realized that these were grown women essentially working on dolls.

Run, a voice inside me pleaded. But my body bypassed this voice and walked me into the main office. I had committed to doing this. I needed to do this—and to see, once and for all, if by empowering myself with the skills necessary to understand the mysterious beauty business I'd started, I could turn things around.

A burly woman named Jo ushered me to a cubicle, and I tried not to judge her—or the rest of the instructors I had passed. I knew it was obnoxious and superficial of me to disapprove of their cropped bright-red dye jobs, their thin penciled brows, and their general *lack* of beauty.

I mean, I certainly wasn't trendsetting with my nude gloss and mascara, but this was beauty school, and these people were the teachers. Why didn't they *attempt* to look current?

A young slim man with dark hair entered, filling the room with a tobacco stench, and took a seat at his desk. Sai, I assumed. "Okay, then." He sat, shuffled, and stapled papers. "We have a *lot* to fill out. I'll need this form and this form, and this form..."

Twenty minutes later, I was finished. "What else?" I asked.

"That's it," Sai said. "You're all done." Now what the hell was I supposed to do for the next two hours and forty minutes? "You can go on break, if you want."

And never come back, the voice sounded again. I ignored it and drove to the mall down the road to kill some time. I called home to Julia as I made my way into a store.

"Hi, babe. How was school today?"

"Good. When are you coming home?"

"Not till late. Daddy is going to put you to bed, okay?"

"*Okay*. But I want you to."

"I know. It won't be forever. Just the next two months."

She was quiet. I didn't blame her. Two months sounded way worse out loud than it had on paper. Jon said hello, and though I wanted, at the sound of his familiar voice, to vent about the nonsense that had just occurred, I didn't dare. This was my own private madness I needed to work through.

Why was I doing this again? Oh, yeah, to help the store.

As I sorted through tops and tried one on in the dressing room, another thought occurred to me. Was I actually trying to throw a Hail Mary, or was I punishing myself? That was entirely possible, too. Punishing myself for starting the stores and having bad ideas. Punishing myself for having become powerless in my own marriage and my own life.

I got back in my car and sat in the parking lot for a bit. My body wouldn't move. I supposed even it had a threshold. *All right, come on*, I tried to coax it. *It's not that bad. It's makeup school. Not prison*. My body wouldn't budge. I lifted my finger—all it would allow—and typed "inspirational quotes" into Google on my phone, a little trickery to bypass my emotions.

"What lies behind us and what lies ahead of us are tiny matters compared to what lies within us," Ralph Waldo Emerson told me. Somehow that got my body out of the car.

"Go and have a seat," Sai said, ushering me into the make-up room, a ten-by-twelve space with about eight classroom desks and one long counter, atop of which was affixed a six-foot-wide mirror surrounded by bulbous, Hollywood-style dressing room lights.

I stood there, the only other person besides him. "Where are the others?" I asked.

"Oh, this is it." He sat behind a teacher's desk and tapped papers into a neat pile. His large brown eyes were the kind that didn't blink, and worse, refused to look away from mine. I took a seat opposite him in a child's desk. With no choice, other than to be blatantly rude—or maybe *to* be blatantly rude—I stared back. "Class starts at six sharp and ends at nine-thirty," he said, transforming into an authoritarian school administrator before my eyes. "You cannot be late. If you are late it will be deducted from your hours. If you fail to meet the eighty-four hours you will have to pay extra to make up the time—"

"Wait. What?" That rule was preposterous. "What if I'm... sick?"

He scowled like a teacher who doesn't acknowledge a voice unless a hand is raised. "You are allowed to miss no more than eight hours or two classes. These are the rules of the Sophia Louise School of Makeup and they are non-negotiable..."

I wanted to laugh, but it was becoming ever less funny, as he went on to deliver the no drug policy, growing sterner with each rule doled out. This was his moment to shine, I understood, maybe the moment he looked forward to all week.

"There are no drugs allowed whatsoever on campus at any time. No sneaking off to take a toke in the bathroom. No quick little hit in the parking lot. No drag off a joint on the drive here or there—"

"So, I'm guessing shooting up in the bathroom is out?" I couldn't help myself.

"Onto the curriculum," he plowed. "We follow the curriculum as it is mandated by the state. First we will cover the anatomy and physiology of the face..."

I began to imagine the homework. *Circle where you see the eyes, the nose, and the lips.* I bit my lip.

"Following that chapter, you will learn to approach eyebrows..."

Learn to *approach* them? I enacted a scene in my head: me and a set of eyebrows sitting at a bar. *Why, hello,* I said. *What brings you guys to a place like this?*

"From there you will learn how to do a full-face makeup application."

Well, we wouldn't want to leave foreheads or chins out of the deal.

"Do you have any questions?"

Yes. Do I get my prison garb now or later?

In the bathroom, I splashed cold water over my wrists. My hands shook. My brain revolted. *Get out of this place now.* But I couldn't. I wouldn't. I was doing this. I had to. *Because what if, in that one-in-a-million chance, my ideas sank into the basket?* What if legitimately, I could make money at the store, recoup our investment, become the hero of our household, and have Jon look at me once again like I was the cat's meow? I opened a stall door, sat down, and looked up. Attached to the back of the door was a sign:

Attention. This is not to be used to throw dirty sanitary napkins or dirty toilet paper in. It is to provide you with a paper bag to place these items in and then place them into the wastepaper container. If we continue to find sanitary napkins and toilet paper we will remove this container.

Well, that didn't make any sense. Take the container out and then people would just throw the sanitary napkins straight onto the floor.

Another sign: *Please respect those of us that go before you and wipe the seat dry if you miss. Place all paper in the waste basket not on the floor. Thank you in advance for your cooperation.*

What kind of animals were these cosmetologists?

And yet, I understood their need for rebellion in this place.

An hour later class was finally scheduled to begin. I shuffled into the makeup room and sandwiched myself between the other two students, both twenty-something women—one, an attractive blonde with a heavy Russian accent; the other, a brunette with billowing cascades of silky hair and a face scarred by acne. We introduced ourselves, and I couldn't help wondering what their lives were like, and what had brought them to this point in time, but mostly I was curious why they hadn't been at orientation. I learned that they'd come to

146

orientation a week earlier. Sai had delivered it. I swallowed down my annoyance just as the teacher entered. She was young, maybe eighteen or twenty years old, on the short and stout side with a spiked, black pixie cut. Her eyes were rimmed with thick black eyeliner. Cinched around her neck was a black leather dog collar.

She drew on the chalkboard "Miss Giana" in fancy script and then took a seat at that same teacher's desk where Sai had enjoyed his fifteen minutes of verbal sadism. She introduced herself by describing her own astonishment at being there, detailing how becoming a makeup artist only one year earlier had led her to this highly respected position of "teacher." A position she was still pinching herself over.

"Even my mother can't believe it, you know what I'm sayin'?" Though I knew exactly what she was *sayin'*, I wished for her own sake she'd stop sayin' it and realize this was the type of information she should probably keep to herself.

"You catch my drift?" was another phrase peppered into her monologue.

Again, I "caught it," but to keep myself rooted in place, when all I really wanted to do was bolt for the door, I tabulated how I planned to divvy up the eight hours I was allowed to miss by leaving an hour early each night for the next two weeks. The thought gave me some relief, so that by the time Miss Giana handed out the *Beauty Essentials 101* handbooks, I was ready to face "Chapter One: Sanitary Conditions."

We didn't delve far into the text before Miss Giana launched into a cautionary tale about nail salons and eyelash glue; apparently she'd contracted an eye infection from the poor conditions under which she'd had fake lashes applied, and learned, to her horror, weeks later, when trying to remove the lashes, that her technician had used hair-weave glue.

I was still reeling from the visual of her pus-encrusted lashes when she held up mascara wands. "These are your best friends. You catch my drift?" She explained we were never to use the wand that came with a mascara tube, but rather, to use these disposable wands. "Some people cut off the tip so they don't get tempted…"

That not only seemed like a good idea for applying makeup to another, but one I planned to make sure the makeup artists at the store were employing when they tested the makeup on themselves. A calm washed over me as I recognized a positive benefit to being there. It dissipated just as quickly.

"…Even though," Miss Giana continued, lowering her voice to a confidante's whisper, "if you wanna know the truth, mascara's probably the one makeup that it's kind of okay to reuse on people. I mean eyelashes don't have germs, you know what I'm sayin'?"

"They do if someone has ocular herpes," I blurted, my mouth bypassing my brain.

"Ocula whatta?" Miss Giana said, stunned.

"I never heard of such a thing," the Russian said.

"Me either," the brunette said.

"Where did you even come up with that?" Miss Giana said.

The world outside of this classroom, I almost blurted, but cupped my mouth in time, fearing what else might come out.

"Oh, look, it's already break time," Miss Giana said. "Just so you guys know, you can bring snacks for break time." Break time? Couldn't we just forgo that and cut the class short? I asked Miss Giana the question. "Oh, no. There is required break time. It's mandated by the Sophia Louise School of Makeup."

Reluctantly I made my way to the vending machine, where I learned from the Russian that leaving early counted as a missed class. I purchased an emergency Snickers bar, and wondered what this Sophia Louise's problem was, and why she was such a stickler for random rules.

"So?" Jon asked when I walked in that night.

"It was…you know…makeup school."

He waited for me to crack, but I couldn't admit defeat so early. I wouldn't allow myself to be defeated so early.

I lasted forty-five minutes into class two.

Miss Giana was describing eye shapes and eye shadow shapes to complement those eye shapes. And then she said this: "So when the eyes are chinky you have to draw in the shadow like this…"

"Come on," I blurted. "You can't say that."

"What?" She turned from the chalkboard.

"I know what she means," the Russian said.

"Yeah, I get it," the brunette said.

"Uh…it's a racial slur," I said, trying to keep my tone somewhat cordial.

"No, it's not," Miss Giana said. "Chinky. You know what I'm sayin'?" She placed her index fingers on the outer corner of her eyes and pulled back the skin. "Chinky."

That's when my body took over, picked me up, and walked me out of the room.

But *what if*…I convinced myself to try another school and audited one a few towns away? It was affiliated with The Makeup Designory School in Manhattan, which already sounded more normal. The instructor, in her fifties, with an artsy bob of black hair and signature red lips, was a television makeup artist with extensive work experience at the top of her field—also better. There were three other students—two over the age of thirty, so I also didn't feel so ancient this time around. Our first assignment was to shade a cylinder from light to dark, aka the way a cheekbone would be colored in with makeup. I shaded mine in, feeling better about the curriculum here too, even managing to convince myself I was making art.

I kept telling myself this, somehow finished the two-month program, and earned the certificate. I brought my makeup kit to the store and started working on the women there, who clearly wanted help, who needed help. It wasn't the worst thing in the world to be needed.

These strange powders and creams and goo mystified them; they admitted their struggles to find the right lipstick colors, the right way to apply foundation. I showed them tricks I'd learned—nude liner on the waterline would open their eyes and make them look less tired; cream blush was a better choice for mature skin; foundations with sunscreens would show up white in photos.

Some days I even pretended their faces were blank canvases, and that creams and powders and shadows were the palettes, the makeup brushes my paint brushes.

"You're a master," one woman said, admiring her face.

"This is your calling," another said, handing me a ten-dollar tip.

This is when I viscerally understood what it was like to be Jon, to feel above a situation and superior to the world around him. I also understood what a hamster might feel like, running on her wheel, because for all my plans and machinations, sales had barely budged. What I *had* managed to do successfully was take over the little business the young makeup artists (whom my sister finally fired) had been doing, so that clients started booking with *me*—something I hadn't fully thought through. Yes, I'd wanted to learn about makeup to bolster sales, to gain a sense of control, and generally understand this business I'd started, but I hadn't banked on greeting the sunrise on weekend mornings while en route to bridal suites.

"Can you be there by six a.m. at the latest?" the bride would inevitably ask as I finished applying her lashes for her trial makeup.

I couldn't say no; I'd done the bridal trial, I had to be the one to show up on her special day at Temple Haverem. I also worried that I'd only had a few months of training. Didn't this bride deserve someone more qualified?

"I absolutely love it." She studied her reflection. "This is the best trial I've had, and I went to two places before you."

And so on weekends, I would throw my hair into a ponytail and tiptoe past Julia's room, hating she'd wake without me, or that I'd miss her cheerleading. I felt even worse about the recent picture she'd drawn of a set of eyes; the lids were painted in blue marker, and the caption read: "make up is not emportant [sic]." Even she knew better than her mom.

One dawn, I set up my kit on a cocktail table near the window of a banquet room at a wedding hall, and worked on one girl after another, desperately coaxing myself to keep my eye on the big picture. If not for the store (that might not be helped), then I needed to focus for my life, or my marriage, or my way back to myself. I was helping to beautify women, I tried telling myself; I was out in the world. I was interacting with people and earning some money. These were positive things. *Right?*

My last client, a vivacious young woman, sat down in the chair. "I'm all yours," she said, in what had become a common theme of women surrendering to a makeup artist.

I began with eyelid primer, something I hadn't known of just a few months earlier, but something that had become as necessary to me in this new world as breathing.

"So did you always want to be a makeup artist?" the girl asked.

And there rushed in that voice again. Loud and clear, the one I'd been hearing since makeup school. *Leave now.* This time it was unwilling to be ignored. *No, I didn't always want to be a makeup artist. I don't even want to be one right now!*

She fluttered open her eyes at my silence. "Um, no, not always," I managed, pretending to concentrate on foundation strokes. "What do you do?" I deflected.

"Voiceovers." She closed her eyes again. "I never thought I could make a career out of something I love, but I feel very fortunate to have made a living for as long as I have."

She looked so serene. So proud of herself. And she should be! Voiceovers sounded fun and cool, and more importantly, what she had always wanted to do.

I came home and unwrinkled seven hundred dollars from my jean pockets. I wanted to be grateful for this burst of cash, and maybe I would have been, if the word prostitution hadn't popped into my head.

Around this time, I would rendezvous for coffee with the writer, Lorna, again. "How's your writing going?" she asked, lifting to her lips a white ceramic mug of French Roast. I told her that the writing was, well...what writing? I was now doing makeup. "Just stop it," she told me, clanking down her cup. She waited for me to say I was kidding.

Unfortunately, I wasn't, I told her, but I was hoping it all might parlay into something better. "Some days I try to think I'm creating art, you know?"

"Listen to me," she said. "Makeup is *not* an art form, so don't even kid yourself. You need to stop this immediately. It does something to the brain when you do something that is not your higher purpose."

I nodded in stunned silence as the truth of her words flattened me. So much for my Hail Mary shot. *Now what?*

Now what turned out to be a little white round of joy called Alprazolam, and another one called Diazepam, both of which I'd found in the medicine cabinet that winter when I was searching for some Tylenol PM. Why had I never encountered these little heavenly gems of relaxation before?

They were Jon's—his doctor had prescribed them following the Lehman crash. He'd taken one or two at most, as he wasn't an "altered state of consciousness" type of guy. But sometimes altered state of consciousness was the place to be, especially when reality wasn't working out as planned.

Hello, anesthetizing, muscle-relaxing, clouds of happiness! Goodbye, seedlings of anxiety!

"Heather, I can't take her to a birthday party Saturday just so you can do one makeup job—this doesn't make any sense."

Not a problem. I might not even go in to work today. Or possibly ever again! Let both stores burn to the ground for all I care. In the meantime, I will be taking a little white cloud hiatus this afternoon. And up and away I went, floating above these trivial arguments, to that cushy place in the ceiling where nothing could dent my happiness.

Now what was also spending more and more time on wine play dates with my girlfriends and being a little European about starting early. It may be only three p.m. on Long Island, but it was five p.m. somewhere. And that meant time for chips and guacamole and organic red wine and laughs, and lots of cynicism.

Now what was also walking through the self-help aisle of Barnes & Noble and realizing that while the shelves were packed, there was nothing there for me anymore, save perhaps for the slew of divorce memoirs—tale after tale of people finding themselves and rebuilding their lives *after* marriage. There were still no linear tales of unblemished, enduring true love, let alone marriages, I noted. And for good reason, I'd finally come to learn. Divorce had a much more appealing narrative arc: believe in the fairy tale, go for it, get burned, and *maybe* get out alive while you still can. As for the self-empowerment texts—books on healing and forgiveness, personal power tomes, and new-age books—they couldn't help me. As much as I had resisted Jon's cynicism over the years, I had somehow grown more cynical myself. As I perused titles, I couldn't help but hear his voice as my own. *Are you really going to read that crap?*

No, I wasn't. Not anymore. A lot of it was sludge, silly sludge, especially a book my sister had given me at some point over the last year called *Mama Gena's School of Womanly Arts.* I'd skimmed along until I got to the chapter that suggested I sit on a mirror and go to town reconnecting with my vagina.

Did I try it? Of course I did. Did it turn me into a goddess my husband could not resist? Of course not. But it did make me consider making a plastic surgery appointment to talk about reconstructive options.

Now what was also accepting that my skin would never get better, and not even caring about it, but rather disconnecting from my body and watching my epidermis take on a life of its own.

Now what was throwing in the towel.

"The less communication you have, the better. Too much talking allows more fodder for argument."

- S.R., Seacliff, married eleven years

"Communicate what you love about your partner and what you want, rather than what you don't want. Example: 'I love when you throw out the garbage,' rather than, 'you never throw out the garbage, asshole.'"

- J.F., Massapequa, married seven years

ROYAL COUNSEL

It was official, I decided one morning as I sat in the den and stared at the frozen backyard. Mission finally complete. It had been a long, circuitous route to get there, but I'd finally done it. Not only had I matriculated into the suburban mainstream, I'd become the person I once puzzled over: a Long Island housewife stuck in a lackluster marriage.

Nice job, Heather.

I had tried everything I could think of to regain a shred of who we had been as a newlywed couple—and who I'd been—which at its very least had been a normalized human being with a sense of liberation and independence. And where had I landed? On the couch at ten a.m., trying to transcend my existence with Xanax, which was, incidentally, wearing off...

I wanted to stay in the cushiness and continue to float. Because that is what I missed most from my marriage, after all, wasn't it? The euphoria that had come with the love.

We had met at that place where we'd both hovered above the stresses and banalities of life, and where he'd looked at me like I was the center of the world. *You would make me the happiest man in the world if you would say yes.*

It was almost laughable to think about—as laughable as my

own thoughts about marriage had been. What was it I'd said? Something about taking our love ride to its highest point? More like shackling iron chains to our ankles and jumping into the deep abyss.

I peeled myself from the couch and headed for the medicine cabinet. Then stopped. I knew better. Pills and wine—like love—also had their initial lift-off period; once their temporary levitations wore off, there was no getting back to the initial high anyway. Well, at least I wouldn't become a drug addict. Although, there were plenty of other ways to perform the clichéd role of unhappy housewife. I poured myself a cup of coffee and Googled therapists in the area.

Judith was in her fifties, a clinical therapist who specialized in family counseling. She wore a neat blonde bob, loafers, and a cardigan. Her office, overlooking Main Street in Oyster Bay, seemed as plain Jane as her with its wooden desk, three ferns, armchair for her, and black leather couch for me.

"So I guess I should ask you what has brought you here today," she said, pulling from a microwave a cup of hot water for her teabag. She offered me some; I declined.

"You mean besides that my marriage reminds me of the ass scene in that Jack Nicholson film, *About Schmidt*?"

"I don't think I'm familiar with that ass scene," she said, and I knew we would get along fine.

I recalled for her that moment in the film when Jack Nicholson's wife bends down looking for something in the refrigerator, and his character stands behind her watching the spread of her bottom that has apparently become amorphous and unmanageable over the years, and is kind of *just there*—like him and their relationship.

"Go on," she said. I went on. And on. Once a week, for a month, I talked a stream to bring her up to date. "I can offer you tools," she said, at the opening of our fifth session.

"What you do with them—what you both do with them—that will be up to you."

Tools sounded like more work. Wasn't there an easier way to fix things, like snapping my fingers or climbing into a time capsule or just showing up at her office?

"Unfortunately, you're both entrenched in the behaviors that took you years to create. You need to employ these tools to even begin to promote positive change."

Her first tip was for me to stop inciting the arguments. Instead of saying, "You're being unreasonable," I should say, "I am feeling like you are mad at me." Or instead of saying, "Don't talk to me like that," I was to say, "It really hurts my feelings when you use that tone."

I went home and waited for the ripe moment. It came during lunchtime while Jon searched the pantry for crackers to accompany the chicken salad he'd bought for himself, refusing to eat my antibiotic-free Nayonaise-style brand. "I can't find my Wheat Thins." He dug through the shelves. "I thought they were right here."

"I'm feeling like you are mad I threw them out."

He swiveled. "Why the F would you throw them out?"

Judith gave me homework assignments.

"Listen to this," I said to Jon as he was changing a high-hat lightbulb in the living room. "People who stay married live four years longer than people who don't."

"Know who else lives longer?" He strained to twist in the bulb. "Men whose wives hold ladders for them. Do you mind?"

I hugged the ladder and kept reading. "I want you to take this test."

"*Heath*."

"Jon, *I'm* going to therapy and reading the books. The least you can do is answer a question."

"I'm listening," he sang, motioning for me to hand him the next lightbulb.

"I can name my partner's three best friends."

"Seriously?"

"Just answer." He named five. "I can list my partner's three favorite movies."

"*Shawshank Redemption, Goodwill Hunting...Gladiator?*"

"I forgot about how much I loved *Gladiator*! Good one. Okay. I can tell you some of my partner's life dreams."

"To live on the beach. To own an organic farm. To stop worldwide factory farming."

"Not bad. How about this? We're on a deserted island. We can only keep ten things from this list: ten gallons of water, pots, pans, a gun with six bullets, one fifth of whiskey..."

"One fifth of whiskey?"

Even I had to roll my eyes—internally, of course; no way I would let him see me give up so easily. Who needed one fifth of whiskey on a deserted island? More importantly, how were these questions helping anyone accomplish anything?

"The questions are aimed at trying to understand your partner," Judith said. "People grow apart in a marriage. Who they once married isn't necessarily who they are married to anymore, and sometimes you have to rebuild the bridge to learn about each other. I wouldn't give up so quickly."

I propped myself on the bathroom counter as he shaved.

"True or False?" I said.

"False."

"I haven't even asked you yet."

"Go ahead."

"What goes wrong is often not my responsibility..."

"Definitely true."

"Be serious. I think my partner can be totally irrational..."

"Is 'often' a choice?"

"And you're perfect?" I shot back.

He buzzed the edge of his beard. "How's that therapy going?"

"It's better than not going," I said.

But was that even true? Despite Jon's ridicule, I was beginning to realize there was a problem inherent in counseling. Having committed to this once-a-week routine, I felt obligated to show up and to talk about something, aka complain about something, even when I was short on negative material.

How's it going? It's fine. Well…actually, now that you mention it, I guess, there was this one moment this week that sucked. Let me tell you all about it in detail and possibly hyperbolize to give it some color and juiciness, so I can relive it and get mad about it all over again.

I reminded myself that Judith wanted to help me. Right? *Sometimes* would be my honest answer. Other times I couldn't help but wonder if she was going through her own monotonous mundanity in life. Showing up for her duties, doling out the wisdom—all the while secretly dreaming about that trip to Tahiti where she would take a long sabbatical and finally write that book she was always talking about.

Had I picked a mediocre therapist, after all? Or was marriage counseling with only one partner present impossible? Especially when the therapist and the client were both women. Two women in a room—I don't know. Even though one was a professional therapist, it kind of went out the window, and some days the session took on the tone of men-bashing.

Or maybe—as much as I hated to admit it—Jon was right: there were no answers there.

Julia turned seven that spring, and I turned forty-three. Both were pivotal ages, but mine seemed like a no-bullshit age. If I was ever going to get back to the authentic me— whoever *she* was —then it seemed like now or never.

The good news was I had spring in my corner and could use to my advantage the sprigs of green and the feeling of a fresh start. Maybe I'd get out and start walking again. The bad news was that my skin was on fire and it hurt just to put on clothes.

I didn't think it was possible, but the ratio of bad skin to good skin had become one to one. The worst part? The disease had finally moved to my face. For close to twenty-five years, my face was one area the disease had spared, but now my lips were betraying me. And they hurt. All winter they had remained raw and itchy. I had lathered them with every conceivable natural product, but even as the balmier weather moved in, they continued to itch so badly I had to apply ice cubes.

"Look at this," I showed Jon. "They're puffing up like slugs."

He examined them and shrugged. "They're chapped lips, Heather. I wouldn't make such a big deal about it."

"I think it's more than that."

"Well, I don't know why you're using coconut oil. You need good old-fashioned Chapstick."

"Like this?" I extracted the black tube from my pocket, shocking him, but also showing him my true desperation— that I'd resorted to petroleum wax.

"I have just what you need." He headed up the stairs and rifled through drawers. He returned with a small round metal tin, the size of a half-dollar, which he placed in my palm.

I examined the worn label. "How old is this?"

"Just trust me. This stuff will get rid of the worst chapped lips. Skiers use it."

"Skiers?" In nine years together, we had never skied a single day. Clearly this was from his pre-Heather bachelor days in Killington, Vermont. I opened the tin and smelled it.

"Heather, it's completely benign. Even if it's expired, the worst that can happen is that it's ineffective."

I dipped my ring finger in and lathered it on. The burning sensation was instantaneous, and I foolishly waited a few minutes to see if it would go away. "Fuck! Jon! This is killing me!" I ran to the bathroom to wash it off. When I was done, my lips looked three times their size. "Great! Now I look like I got Juvederm injections."

He tried to hold it in but burst out laughing.

"It's not funny, Jon!"

"It's kind of funny."

A few days later, the swelling appeared around my eyes. I woke up to find my crow's feet puffed up, and under my left eye, a red patch of skin the size of a plum. I sat on the white wax paper at the dermatologist's office and listened to him reprimand me for not taking his advice on popping the methotrexate pills months earlier.

"I don't know what you are waiting for," he said, tilting my chin toward the light while he inspected my lips. "Things just don't get better on their own." He had a point. And yet trying everything under the sun didn't always work either. He clicked off the light. "Well, it's not psoriasis."

I sat up. "Then what is it?"

"Hard to say. It's definitely some kind of flare up. But not facial psoriasis. It looks like some kind of contact dermatitis. Possibly an allergy. It could be that you're coming into contact with something that is causing an allergic reaction."

Could that something be a little institution called marriage?

"Come back and see me in a few days," he said, "and, in the meantime, try not to introduce anything new to your routine."

I went to the pharmacy and filled the prescription for a steroid cream. The swelling subsided and left my face burned and my eyes and lips encircled with dried red rings.

"Mom, are you okay?" Julia asked as I air-kissed her goodnight.

"I'm fine," I lied. "Don't worry."

Meanwhile, I walked past mirrors, unable to recognize myself. Eventually, I stopped looking, not wanting to see this creature from the black lagoon. I was afraid to touch anything. Afraid to leave the house.

"Maybe it was the hand cream I used at the store," I wondered aloud to Jon as we sat on the couch in front of the television. "Or the cashews in my salad at The Cheesecake Factory. Look at the picture of this guy's face." I swiveled my laptop so he could see a man in Costa Rica, his face ballooned like a pufferfish; he'd apparently eaten mango, which was a sister species to cashews, and had immediately blown up.

Jon paused the remote on Brian William's face. "What?"

"Doesn't this look identical to what I have?"

"But you're not even allergic to nuts. Just go to a *doctor*."

"My doctor has no answers."

"Then go to another one."

"Doctors don't always have the answers, Jon."

"No, but the internet does?"

"Enough," I said and swigged water. Between my inflamed skin and swollen face, between us never having been able to "move forward" or get back to our love, my threshold could hold no more.

He kept going. "All I'm saying, Heather, is that you need to speak to someone real…"

It began to crawl over me, what felt akin to hatred, something I'd yet to experience with Jon. Frustration? Yes. Boredom? Yes. Exasperation? Hell, yes.

But never hatred. It devoured me from head to toe like an army of flesh-eating beetles. His lack of sympathy. His insistence that he knew best.

The right way.

"But no, you'd rather obsess over…I don't know what. Looking at ridiculous photos of strangers who live halfway across the world who have none of the same symptoms as you…"

I tightened my grip around my glass, feeling the need to

smash something, feeling the need to to throw my glass of water at his head, feeling the need for sympathy, feeling the need for *his love*. "Jon, I said *enough!*"

He eyed me. He had never seen me look at him like that. His surprise jarred my own mind. *Feeling the need for his love?* What a dumbass I'd been this whole time. When the trick, the key, the answer had *nothing to do with him.*

I stood there feeling the full light of the epiphany wash over me. All this time, I'd been looking to him to show me— as he had done during our honeymoon phase—how much he loved, respected, and validated me. All this time, I'd been looking to him for help in returning us to the feeling of euphoria. All this time I'd been trying to see myself once again through his loving eyes. What was it I'd said about love? It was about the way another made us feel about ourselves.

Well, scratch that.

What mattered was seeing myself with love. And maybe it wasn't about finding myself, as much as it was about *remembering* myself—and selves—all of them.

The twelve-year-old girl who had looked in the mirror and known who she was and had acted accordingly—*that* was power to me. When my actions had been aligned with who I was at my core and I'd been doing exactly what I needed to be doing, which was really accepting myself for who I was at any given time—hard, sharp, soft, or round—that was power. Whether I stayed at home or went to work, so long as I self-respected—that was power.

I didn't need to conquer the world, and I certainly didn't need to do things to win his love back. I just needed to be and to *enjoy* this existence.

"All I'm saying," Jon tried again, "is that if you were on this side of things…"

"Stop," I said.

"I'm just trying to get you to see…"

My hand flew up again and amazingly, he quieted. What

was it a friend said to me over wine once? Men are like dogs, and you have to keep pushing them down.

Stop them at level one, I believe were her words. *Don't wait for them to rise to level ten.*

Another dumbass move on my part. If marriage had been reinforcing our roles, I'd not only allowed my "king" to grow into "the patriarchy" but to rise to a tyrannical level ten.

"Here's the deal," I said. "You can have your opinions about what I should do with my skin, but I can't listen to them. I won't listen to them. I need to get *myself* through this health crisis."

And instead of throwing my glass at him, I drained it of delicious alkaline "bullshit" water that he didn't believe in. Well, *I* did. Kind of.

Regardless, there was no need to be thirsty while having my breakthrough.

"Be honest with yourself."
- *R.G., Melville, married fourteen years*

ABLUTIONS

"Testing for allergies is a bit like detective work," the nurse practitioner at the Asthma and Allergy Institute said, perusing my intake form. "We're going to have to really pay attention to the clues."

The night before I'd woken up with the swollen face, I'd had two anesthetizing glasses of wine, but that certainly hadn't been anything new. Harriet and Stan had been visiting, and we'd played cards. I'd made shrimp and peas over rice—all foods I'd eaten before. And if the shrimp had been bad, they all would have woken up swollen too.

Jon and I had also argued, but again, nothing new, unless you count that it was in front of Harriet and Stan. (I'd started to theorize that if it took eighteen months for romance to fade in a marriage, then it took a little more than double that time for the good behavior to end with the in-laws.)

"It's not easy," Harriet had offered, packaging up the leftover rice in an old Chinese food container she had brought up from Cherry Hill. "But you know what they say the secret formula of staying together is."

"What's that?"

"Not divorcing."

Some formula, I remembered thinking, especially in light of the icy comments and doors slamming that had gone on between her and Stan that morning.

"So we will start with full blood work," the nurse cut into my thoughts. "We'll check the nut profile." She penciled off small square boxes on a sheet of paper. "Then the animal profile—dander and all of that. Molds, pollens, gluten, eggs, soy, wheat, dairy. We'll also check your cholesterol, thyroid, and see if your immune antibodies are in order. This will be step one. Step two, we can start with the patch test system, where we test the cosmetics profile. Shall we do our exam?"

She pulled back my paper gown. "You poor thing," she said, referring to the patches of psoriasis climbing over my ribcage.

"I've learned to live with it," I said, wondering if that was actually even true anymore.

What I'd learned to accept was that I'd been the unlucky one between my brother, sister, and I who had inherited it from my father. When the father is the carrier, one out of three children will get it. When the mother is the carrier one out of five children will get it. And while I used to buy into all sorts of ridiculous things like I'd been the chosen one, because I was spiritually stronger than my siblings, or they wouldn't have been able to deal with the disease. I knew as I sat on the exam table that I'd never been stronger than them and maybe not even less lucky. If anything, my psoriasis had to do with inheriting most of my father's genes and possibly also about my relationship with him. That first dime-sized spot had appeared on my forearm when I was at a major emotional roadblock with him.

The same obstacles I was confronting in my marriage?

I stepped off the scale, my mind loosening, as parallels formed in front of me. I'd been accepting my skin outbreaks all these years as residual symptoms from my childhood, but what if they weren't residual? What if they were fresh? New wounds for this old emotional material I hadn't quite mastered?

A chance to learn and grow. And not only with Jon, but in all my relationships. The abandoned, motherless me, the middle-child-pleaser me, had been seeking validation not just from my husband, but from friends, siblings, Jon's kids, Harriet and Stan, customers, the person who held the door open at CVS…pretty much *everyone* I came in contact with.

"Deep breath," she directed, moving a stethoscope to my

back. I inhaled, feeling like there was no more denying the connection between my body and mind or that one could influence the other; I had to learn self-validation. But what of these *new* symptoms? What message could be had there? "While we wait for the blood results, take this antihistamine. I usually don't like to prescribe these as they can tend to mask the issue. But you need some relief."

I washed it down with water and waited. But apparently there was no more masking to be done.

Over the next few days, the relief was slight at best. Afraid to leave the house, I turned on my computer and delved back into Cyberspace. I typed in "causes of chapped lips and swollen eyes." If I applied my symptoms to the myriad generic and scholarly articles, the possibilities of diseases I could be dying from were endless. Getting nowhere, I thought of lobbing the question out to the Universe, but after the last debacle, I was having a hard time summoning belief that this would help. Whether Jon's cynicism had finally become a part of me, or I'd unwittingly grown up somehow, it did suddenly seem a bit silly to think that *if* there was a Universe listening, She, He, Whatever, would communicate through a Word document. Not to mention that this Being, of all time, space, and intergalactic matter, might have more important work to focus on, say, like droughts, wildfires, or world hunger. And yet I reminded myself that my old pleas had once worked—or I at least believed they had—and at this point, I was willing to try anything.

Dear Universe, Could you please let me return to good health and get to the bottom of whatever is going on with my face…

My cell phone interrupted my typing. The nurse practitioner was calling. Well, I'll be! "Good news," she said. "You're not allergic to anything."

"But how can that be?"

"It's hard to say but keep taking the antihistamine and

continue to keep a look out. Don't introduce anything new. We'll see what happens over time." In other words, she had no answers either. I picked up typing where I'd left off....

...Please, I am begging you! Just tell me what the hell it is!

Twenty-four hours later, the universe answered my letter with a big fat yeast infection. I sat on the toilet, considering a new draft to give this Somebody or Something a good piece of my mind. But why bother? Clearly, I had only myself to blame for having taken the antihistamines, which seemed to somehow have sent my system over the edge. Between those pills and the steroid creams, I'd somehow made things worse.

Unless. It was somehow all connected.

Unless my facial swelling had something to do with a yeast infection? I dimly remembered reading something about, what was it...yeast in the intestinal tract?

I scrambled back to my computer, and typed in: Eyes, Lips, Yeast. Systemic. Hundreds of images loaded: pictures of people with facial features blown up like mine.

Were many of these forums and blogs laughable? Of course, they were. But at this point, research and medicine hadn't solved the riddle either, which seemed a common theme for the apparent masses suffering from *candida albicans* overgrowth. I gleaned that there was a delicate balance in the body, a healthy ecosystem of yeast and bacteria. But the balance could be thrown out of whack from medications or foods and when the bacteria level diminished, the yeast flourished, leaving the host to suffer symptoms that seemed very much like mine.

Antibiotics could upset the balance, as could steroids. Other culprits were sugar and alcohol. Basically, my entire self-medicating diet. Jon had been right at least in that I was different when I drank. Supposedly the alcohol fed the yeast, and in turn, the yeast produced even more alcohol. So, two drinks for me was ostensibly more like three or four compared to a person with a balanced digestive tract. I continued through the labyrinth of stories and pictures, sympathetic to the sufferers. Though, seriously, did they have to post their stool samples? And on dinner plates of all things? And yet, what the hell *was* that? Had that tomato-skin stool with dark strings and wormy tentacles really come out of a human being? Would it come out of me?

I couldn't stop reading testimonials either, proclaiming the use of anti-fungal herbal remedies and colon cleanses and diet plans. Some phrasings freaked me out. This one in particular: "Left untreated, this yeast can multiply at a rapid rate." I felt a chill down my spine and suddenly imagined myself like Jon Malkovich in *Being Jon Malkovich*, only instead of human souls having entered a portal into my brain, *Candida albicans* had taken hold of the ship.

But it was when I stumbled upon a well-known functional medicine site and saw the link to "spiritual causes of *Candida* overgrowth," I stood at attention.

Long-term resentment was number one on the list. Was I holding onto resentment? For the first time since the swelling began, I actually laughed out loud. Of course, I was. Seven or eight years of resentment. And it was hurting me more than him. The first step in curing *Candida* overgrowth is to let go of the resentment, the site read.

I leaned back, taking in that profundity, and wondering how. *Curedofcandida7845* suggested the best way was through an intensive colon cleanse using psyllium husk and bentonite clay. From the looks of the acrimonious evidence expelled onto *7845's* porcelain china, I figured he had some expertise.

No one in the mainstream believed me, which was fine, considering I barely believed myself. Like the Epstein-Barr virus, *Candida albicans* overgrowth is one of those periphery diagnoses of hypochondriacs. Alas, I was at least making my way back to the fringe, as I stirred up my husk and clay shakes—a misnomer if ever there was one. That glop was hard to get down. The allergist nurse had at least heard of *Candida* and was even aware of a connection between auto-immune issues and "leaky gut," which allegedly led to yeast overgrowth. She felt, however, that my having it was unlikely because she had tested my blood against molds and fungi. My dermatologist had also heard of *Candida* overgrowth and had even treated it in other patients, but he dismissed the diagnosis. If I had it, he maintained, the corners of my mouth would be cracked and my tongue whitened with thrush.

But to humor me, he gave me a sample of an anti-fungal cream that he normally prescribed for the condition. I rubbed it on my lips and the next morning the chaffed and chapped skin looked almost cured.

"Probably a coincidence," Jon said. Needless to say, he wasn't buying into my "pseudo-science discovery."

But I was past wanting his approval. If he chose not to speak to me during the week I had my mercury filling removed by a biological dentist—in Long Island, not Switzerland—then so be it. If he chose to blow a gasket over the liquid chlorophyll, oregano oil, and caprylic acid capsules, or the probiotics, flax oil, hemp seed oil, cod liver oil, tinctures of burdock root, wormwood, clove, black walnut husk, slippery elm bark powder, saffron, or the Paul D'Arco tea that littered our countertop and refrigerator, that was his prerogative.

When he tried to talk "sense" into me, I validated his feelings and then told him to basically stop wasting his breath. More, I didn't feel the need to sway him to my side. As quirky and quacky as this all seemed, it was my truth. It took about a month, but he eventually stopped resisting. Maybe because the damage to the Amex card had already been done. Or maybe because he couldn't stomach the details of my "truth," like where I was going with that cup of coffee in a glass.

I decided to spare Julia as well.

"Mom, why is there a balloon in the shower?" she asked, referring to the enema bag I'd washed and hung to dry.

The answer, of course, was because a coffee enema would allow my liver and gall bladder to make the "squish" sound that would signal bile production, which would then help flush the intestines for a deep cleanse. But I opted for: "Oh, it's just for my medicine for my skin."

"You put medicine in a balloon?"

"It's kind of a boring story, Jules. You don't really want to hear about it," I said.

"More like traumatizing," Jon said, walking past.

"But effective," I added.

He didn't respond. The proof was in my face. The facial swelling had gone down almost immediately. And by the end of month two, my psoriasis started to clear as well, something I had not seen happen since our wedding. That's when the path back to myself began to clear, somehow reminding me of the book Julia and I had read when she was younger: *We're Going on a Bear Hunt.*

We can't go over it. We can't go under it. We've got to go through it.

There was a lot of mud in life to go through. And apparently even more in the human intestinal tract.

In the blogs and forums, I had read about people experiencing old emotions welling up as they sloughed away the sludge lining the intestinal walls. For me, it felt more like flames licking away at my insides. No sooner would I flush the toilet, my new home away from home, when I would stand in the kitchen and the flames would ignite and start boiling my blood.

How many times had he risen to level ten! And how many times had I let him!

Then, within seconds, a coolness would overtake me, and a soothing balm of lucidity would pour over me as I understood that I had risen to my own unacceptable levels.

While he'd sat idly by, letting me.

After the coolness came the sadness, whooshing through me like old ghosts. All those times—when I had curled

171

myself up during those soft motherhood moments, wanting his attention, perhaps even re-enacting childhood traumas in my adult body—told me there might never be a fix for some wounds, but that just being aware of them was enough to begin the healing process.

After the sadness, came the lightness. The euphoric high I'd been after all this time.

I floated through my house, through the everyday tasks of food shopping, making dinner, carting Julia to soccer, seeing this life, this kitchen, this yellow bell pepper in my hand, as if they were constructs. What was real was my spirit and Jon's and Julia's, the three of us, circling around each other as we set this artificial table, clanking down silverware that seemed like props—pliable, moldable matter—in this spiritual play that was *really* happening.

Driving to and from work and surrounded by people, I started to feel as if I might as well be in an alternate world akin to *The Matrix*. We were all just play acting. The real drama—it was high in the sky somewhere—was soul to soul. Was this what the Buddhist meant by enlightenment? Was this real transcendence?

"It's called not eating," Jon said, when I tried sharing my experience. But I don't think even he was buying his remark. He had started watching me, becoming interested.

"So you're just drinking juices?" he asked. "Nothing else?"

"Just liquids and phytonutrients."

He hedged at phytonutrients but curiosity overcame him. "And you don't need food? You're not starving?"

Food. Who needed it? Food was another prop. I needed water and puréed leaves—if that.

"Well, you do look good." He grabbed his gut. "I need to lose a few."

"You should try it. You'll feel amazing."

"We'll see." He sniffed at my Green Goddess juice.

The realizations came next, one at a time, like a bead of string lights. By chasing my own truth and taking back responsibility for my own happiness, I wasn't cutting Jon out of my life. I was realizing that I had to be my own circles and dots and swirls within *our* painting. Because while I was alone on this journey, I was also choosing to be with him. And the truth was that it was this togetherness struggle within our marriage that had allowed me to evolve.

Without the growth that came from the stresses of building a life and raising a child together, without the discomfort that came from bickering and resistance, without the resentments I had been holding onto, without being married to a strong-willed, almost unbendable partner in our marriage of opposites, without the pain that came from *not getting his love*, I wouldn't have had the opportunity to thicken my skin or to face my own shortcomings.

Maybe *this* was the true meaning and purpose of soulmates, or any mate—not to compliment or coddle each other, not to complete the missing parts for each other, but to push each other to become our better selves, to nudge each other to fill in our own missing gaps.

I had been busy rewriting imaginary chapters to a sequel of Shell Silverstein's *The Missing Piece Meets the Big O*, but I realized I had forgotten half of Silverstein's story.

When the missing piece—a triangle—meets its match (a circle sans a triangular cut-out), it is true that they both click, fulfill the lack in each other, and can roll along happily. But the part I forgot about is that the missing piece begins to grow, and the two find that they are no longer compatible. This is when the Big O rolls in and shows, by example, how the missing piece can simply round off its own edges and roll forward on its own, and if it chooses, to even accompany the Big O.

Still, the two didn't marry.

So I went ahead for kicks and continued constructing in

my head the next chapter title to the domesticated sequel. Chapter Four: *The Missing Piece Completes Herself Regardless of, but also Grateful for her Companion.*

Around this time, I considered the Klimt print again. "That's you and Daddy," Julia had said casually one night as we walked by the picture, which still hung in our bedroom. I'd harrumphed, stuck on the idea that Gustav had never married and therefore never experienced the struggle of domestic entanglement. But later that night, I'd looked up at the painting again and had become lost in critics' interpretations of it.

While most agreed that the painting captured a kind of esoteric love, others maintained that the painting was actually a depiction of the myth of Apollo and Daphne. As the story went, one day Apollo mocked Cupid (or "Eros"). In retaliation, Cupid struck Apollo with an arrow, infusing him with love for the virgin nymph, Daphne, and then struck Daphne with another arrow, filling her with hatred for Apollo. Apollo chased after Daphne, and she begged her father, the river god Peneus, to open the earth to let her escape or to at least change her form. As Apollo caught up to her, Peneus changed his daughter into a laurel tree.

The painting, the critics suggested—evident by the vines that wrapped around the woman's feet and the laurel crown atop the man's head—is said to be that moment when Apollo catches up with Daphne and she morphs into a tree.

Whether the critics were right or not, thinking about that interpretation made me see the painting differently, and see love, not as a constant ideal, but as a fleeting, complex, and sometimes violent concept. One that could be a vehicle for transformation. I'd needed a master class in effective arguing, and Jon needed to learn that there were alternative ways of thinking. I'd needed to consider science and math as a starting point for my endeavors, and he'd needed to consider "pseudo-science"—or at least be open-minded about it. I'd needed to learn how to stand my ground, and he'd needed to learn that you can't win every argument. But it is true that you can't change a person—at least not by preaching at him. He had to come to his own truths.

A few days after sniffing my juice, as I was gathering my keys and pocketbook, he called to me. "If you're going to the store, can you get me a cooler of greens? And some wheatgrass?"

I walked to the doorframe of his office and stared.

"What?" he said.

"Do my ears deceive me?"

"Very funny. But just so you know, I'm going to have protein too. I got some steaks for the freezer. I figure I'll juice during the day and have steak at night."

Atkins style. The science of ketosis. I'd heard his spiel before.

"Don't have steak, Jon. Of all the foods in the world, red meat has the lowest vibrations, not to mention all the hormones and antibiotics…"

"Heath, come on, don't ruin it for me. I'm not ready for vibrations."

One step at a time.

"Of course you can still be a feminist and a housewife...
Define feminism."

- S.M. Muttontown, married nine years

THE CORONATION

I sat in my car at the bus stop drinking homemade almond milk, my absolute new favorite beverage in the world, made with puréed dates, almonds, and coconut, blended with water and a pinch of Himalayan sea salt. It might as well have been a vanilla malted, it was so good. I was also starving. My skin looked great, but my arms and belly had started to go soft, and that worried me, as I had been reading up on the dangers of depletion. Cleansing had its place, but, like everything else, its high was ultimately fleeting.

It was time for me to rebuild and restore—and to find an equilibrium in more ways than one. The body had suddenly become the easy part. Adding healthy "mono" foods back into my diet, a fancy way to describe adding back one food at a time, would be easy, as would adding essential oils like flax seed, coconut, hemp, and cod liver oil. Okay, maybe not that last one, but I'd heard lemon-flavored cod liver oil wasn't so bad.

The difficulty was what to do with my mind, and how to keep myself from slipping back into the negativity. I knew I could not expect more from Jon—especially after the unpredictable, rollercoaster ride of love we'd been on together. Wanting more from him would only leave me disappointed.

I knew that I had to be my own self-contained being, responsible for her own feelings of self-love, because being dependent on Jon's love would only lead to frustration, anger, and ultimately, a letdown.

I knew that my notion of love had changed, just as my definition of soulmates had changed. Where I had once fallen for the kit-and-caboodle of the fairy tale, thinking that this person and our rapturous love would complete me, I now believed that this love had actually been a nudge, or maybe a series of them—to work on completing myself.

But were any of these ideas sustainable? Wouldn't it eventually be impossible for me not to want from my husband? Was it realistic to be *so* self-contained within a marriage? I feared slipping back into my old ways, especially in light of the mind-body connection. Let's say, I added back my mono foods and oils—or worse, slipped back to having an occasional glass of wine or a piece of chocolate—would new feelings of resentment usurp feelings of appreciation? Would my skin crust over and my face swell as the old version of my angry, ugly self reared her head?

I didn't want to lose sight of myself in the mirror again.

Yes, I was different from that granola coffeehouse girl; I was now a bentonite clay-eating woman who refused to leave home without her vitamin bag, but a hopeful and liberated clay-eating woman, and I was scared to lose that feeling that I could float above any level of bullshit and still stay centered.

Make a list, the little voice on my shoulder said. *A happiness list of all the good stuff so that you can connect with it when you feel yourself slipping away.*

Please, said the other being on the other shoulder. *Total fluff!*

But was it fluff? Or was it a way to etch into my brain the things I needed to remember to keep in mind? I waited for bad shoulder voice, my inner cynic, to rebuke the thought. She was silent. With nine minutes before the bus pulled up, I opened Notes on my iPhone and typed furiously.

Lying in bed with Jules was the first thing that came to mind. At night, after reading, when the lights were out, her mind unspooled, and I got to hear the good stuff, like her dreams and concerns, the funny thing her teacher said, the vanilla cupcakes she wanted to make for the last day of school. In that space with her, there was no worry about the housing market or employment.

There was no concern that my marriage might blow up, or my face might swell, or my skin might flare up. Being with Jules was just pure *being*. And there was the realization that, for better or worse, Jon and I were succeeding as a couple teaching *her* how to be—and co-civilizing her. Which led me to add to my list.

Building a family culture. Having a kid wasn't about making someone in our likeness, as I'd initially thought, but raising someone in her own likeness so that she could one day hopefully use that learned culture to get out and do good. Despite our often petty differences, we'd so far managed a culture for Jules that I was proud of, a home base of tolerance and acceptance. A place where, when the question arose, "Mom why do two boys sometimes kiss?" the answer was, "Sometimes boys like boys, and girls like girls. Now can you please pass the salt?" A place where we don't use the word hate (though Jon might add, "unless you're talking about olives"). A place where we at least aim to take the high road, to practice the things we love, and to be considerate of others. A place where we address ageism by pointing out how much we have to learn from our elders, or where we address racism by not focusing on differences in people but on their sameness. A place where feminism has nothing to do with a job title or role but instead a feeling, attitude, belief-system, and the ability to make the choices one wants to make—regardless of what anyone has to say about it, radical feminists included.

There were the five minutes in the morning after the bus pulled away, too, that made me happy—the walk to the top of the driveway.

The ascension. Toward French Roast coffee and also something higher, something better, something waiting for me at the top of some metaphorical hill that I haven't yet discovered, haven't yet created.

Creating. That was happiness to me, too, wasn't it? Not in a

Martha Stewart type of way. I certainly had no desire to sew my own Halloween costumes, but I did enjoy crafting a good meal or sketching alongside Julia or turning out a good sentence—even just a text to a friend that I knew would make her laugh. The high of stringing together the right combination of words could sustain me for hours.

Transforming things. The stores had actually turned out beautifully. It was running them that had been out of my wheelhouse.

Sunshine. On a day like today—a balmy May afternoon—I could lie on the concrete patio, the heat of the stone grounding my spine. I could feel absorbed and also small, insignificant, and vulnerable under the vast blue sky. It gave me that sense of *why not?* Why not try for what you want in life? And also, if you don't want to try for anything, that's okay, too; it will hardly make a difference in the grand scheme of things.

Routine. That could actually be happiness. Yes, it was something I rebelled against, but I also liked knowing that my kid had order and predictability to her day, something I'd craved growing up—the kind of comfort where "no news is good news."

Monogamy. Along the same line of thought, maybe this too needed to make the list. While unnatural in the animal kingdom, we are supposed to be evolved higher beings, after all. Besides, there's something to be said for familiarity and history and even boredom. Boredom is peace. Boredom is not getting a sexually transmitted disease.

Friends. Working and non-working, these women were my village, my tribe, my sounding boards, my exercise, coffee-wine-and-green-juice companions, my liberators from weekday doldrums, my co-conspirators, therapists, and spiritual guides as we hashed out issues with our kings, and in some cases knights, jesters, princes, stewards, royal fools, masters of ceremonies…while they doled out their wisdom.

"Men don't want to hear every detail. They want the bottom

line and then the space to deal with it," one such friend told me recently. "And the best way to do that is to text them."

I put her words to the test, and I thumbed the news to Jon: *I'm working the next three Saturdays in a row. I need you to take her to all her games.*

Instantly, those three floating dots appeared on my screen, signifying that he was reading, only instead of his usual rapid-fire response, silence ensued. A moment later, I heard the ping. *Okay.* And to think that I'd foolishly been standing there all these years in real time, hashing out the details, and absorbing his disappointment. Thank god for friends!

Maturity. As much as I'd resisted, this was happiness too—feeling like I had wised-up in this second childhood of sorts and maybe sharpened my own skill and knowledge set, which I could share with the village. Like positioning the "Hand" for maximum effectiveness.

The trick was to keep the palm vertical and firmly resistant against the air, the way a mime might press it against pretend glass while simultaneously projecting the message, "Be nice."

Because even if marriage was a second childhood, being a wife was also sometimes like being a mother, or maybe more aptly, a queen—one who understands that, while ruling with an iron fist has its place, the Hand, or the flicking of a finger, or even the perfectly timed throwing of a look can be imminently more powerful.

Just a few days earlier, I'd been slicing a zucchini for juicing when Jon entered. "Careful," he'd said. "If you hold the knife like that you might cut yourself."

Really? Micromanaging how a grown woman should cut a vegetable? That might have been my response a mere two months earlier. Now I simply smiled with the message, *Not appropriate.*

He stormed out, of course, but returned a moment later to nibble on vegetables.

I'd started to realize queens also don't explain themselves. That had been part of my problem when it came to our food issues. I'd tried to convince Jon to "invest in his health," replete with links, eventually to university studies, when what I should have been doing was let *him* do the work of accepting that I wasn't budging an inch more on this issue. I'd come as far as I could to meet him on food issues. I'd already asked myself if I could do with less organic produce, and the answer had been, a *little* less. I could consent to conventional thick-skinned fruits and vegetables, but not the "dirty dozen," the thin-skinned fruits and vegetables that absorbed pesticides easier.

Whether my new resolve deterred Jon from pushing back, or whether he'd finally grown tired of the debate himself, I can't say. But he did seem to complain less about it. I decided to reciprocate by zipping my disapproval about his typical food. Even if I was dying when I found a package of Stop and Shop ground round, in all its bloodied gore, occupying space on the pristine refrigerator shelf, I would remind myself that this was his belief (with a note to self to wipe down the shelf afterward with water and vinegar).

I also made a secret pact to keep my own food phobias and issues to myself. Like when I needed to wash the organic cauliflower and it wouldn't fit under my filtered water tap, I covertly cupped the water in my hands and splashed it onto the vegetable. Not fooling anyone.

"You know all you're doing is *not* washing the cauliflower," Jon had said.

This was the moment that I saw the struggle of our marriage distilled, perhaps even the struggle of humanity distilled. We were like two magnets with repelling poles when it came to our core issues, two countries with opposing governments, two religions with contradictory texts. But if we could consciously realign ourselves, if we could at least pretend to honor the other's ideals—or just exercise a little diplomacy—we might not only get along but enjoy each other's existence.

He'd smirked, waiting to see what I would do. I waited to see what I would do. He had, after all, consented to having cauliflower soup as a main meal; it was my turn to at least pretend to be okay with chlorine-laden tap water tainting the pristine vegetable. Luckily, nature offered help with the appearance of a nasty dead fly wedged between two florets. And organic smorganic; there was no way I was eating a bug.

"You're right." I'd feigned a sigh and opened the regular tap, letting the compromised torrents wash away the offending black spec.

The bus rounded the corner, and I typed in my last happiness entry for the afternoon: *Being married to Jon.* He was still the smartest guy I knew, still one of the wittiest people I knew, still one of the most determined and persistent people I knew.

"Preferable equity or mezzanine debt," he was saying into the phone as I returned from the bus and dropped Julia's backpack on the counter.

I walked into his office and sat down on the throne. It had seen better days. The cats had scratched at it until their last old-age breaths, and I was pretty sure our new goldendoodle, Goldie, had been sleeping on it lately, as the seat looked sunken.

"Have you been a bad mush face?" I asked the dog as she sat before me. "Huh? Have you been sleeping in Daddy's royal throne?" She dropped down and exposed her belly.

The chair needed an overhaul, maybe some new upholstery, maybe even a queen's print this time. A cobalt blue Ikat material would look incredible juxtaposed against the dark woodwork of the room.

Jon held his hand over the receiver. "What's up?" he mouthed.

"Want a snack?" I whispered. He nodded enthusiastically. I threw together a hemp seed salad, tossing in a dressing of lemon and olive oil as he entered.

"I didn't know you were eating solid food again."

"I'm afraid to," I said. "But I guess it's time."

"Now you're scaring me." He pulled down bowls and retrieved silverware.

"I don't want my face to blow up again." *And I don't want to be full of anger or resentment either.*

He stabbed the leaves and seeds and gobbled mouthfuls down, happy to have something prepared for him again. I made a mental note that deprivation from time to time wasn't such a bad strategy. "Well, if you see it acting up, can't you just pull back and do...your thing?"

Not his most articulate capitulation, but I caught it. And still, I would need to be careful to check in with my list.

We took our plates into the sunshine and sat on lounge chairs overlooking the grass. "How was your call?" I asked.

"Not great."

"Sorry." The breeze blew up my napkin.

"You know, I was thinking about it this morning. It's just amazing how much life costs."

"Jon," I said, gently. He knew where I was headed by my tone.

"I hear you. But living isn't free. Even in Bumfuck, Florida."

He looked tired, and it was only noon. I decided against re-upholstering the throne in an Ikat print, and instead to buff out the scratches from the six-foot-high carved wooden back and lion paw hands and re-stuff the brown leather seat.

This was who he was; he also needed to believe in his dream and ascension to something higher.

The right way.

"You know, you should be very proud of yourself. I mean it, Jon. Look at this beautiful house. Look at all your past accomplishments. You've given Eddie and Emily an incredible education. You're an amazing father. Not many people can do what you've done so far...I know that your father would be proud of you."

He looked at me. "You think so?"

"Without question."

"Thanks for that."

A hawk circled overhead. He eyed it. "The thing is if I could just get one investor to go first. It really is a great project, and they would make a good return." His eyes were bright and wide. The eyes that were failing him. What was his mind-body connection? Myopia? Self-criticism? Some other residual childhood issues that *he* was reliving afresh in this marriage? He was full of potential. Every deal was full of potential—but also full of pressure and anxiety. I'd read somewhere that the number one regret people have on their deathbeds is that they've worked too hard.

And that's when I felt it. I wanted to love him for all his bad behavior too. He was my husband, my family, my co-culture creator. Sure, he couldn't get out of his own way sometimes, sure his ego blew to incredible widths, but that was only behavior. When Julia behaved badly, I didn't think of abandoning her. I would tell her that her behavior was unacceptable, but I would never think of leaving her.

I wanted to be able to stretch my heart and find the love beyond when he was down and out or feeling hopeless. I wanted to find it when the hair sprung wild and the nastiness spewed and the intolerance for me poured out.

I wanted to give back love in the face of disdain. That's how I would not only keep my skin at bay, but also keep my mind intact—and maybe even keep my marriage successful. I couldn't make promises. But it was a new ideal to which I could aspire, wasn't it? A lofty, worldly ideal. For wasn't this the real purpose and meaning of true love—and of marriage?

To learn to love unconditionally, to give when you don't get, to send beams of love to your offender, like the store clerk who gives you an attitude, or the person who steals your parking spot, or the country that threatens to nuke you.

All right, maybe that last one was pushing it. Or was it? Couldn't marriage be a sort of microcosm of two nations needing to figure out how to share the same real estate of planet Earth? Maybe we all just needed to give the love instead of trying to get it. Or ask not what your marriage can give to you but what you can give to your marriage.

"Jon, and I mean this, you really are the most extraordinary man I have ever met. And you're the smartest person I've ever met, not to mention the funniest, most handsome, protective and loyal person."

"That's sweet, Heath, but—"

"It's true," I said, meaning it. I jumped in his lap and threw my arms around him. "You can do this. It's going to work."

"You think so?" He looked at me, hopeful, and I not only believed my words, I believed in us. I saw sparks of our original connection again and the way I'd been drawn to him for the missed mother culture he offered. And how he'd been drawn to me for the paternal inspiration I'd offered.

Whether we'd been ordained and split at our spiritual birth or just biological beings who'd liked each other's pheromones and had spiked each other's dopamine, mattered little now. We were married, making the choice to be *lifemates*, which was way more impressive. It was why people deserved congratulations for hanging in there. Marriage was not the culmination of love, not the endpoint of a ride, but the beginning of it. Meeting a mate was the easy part. Staying with that mate...maybe *that* was the real definition of soulmates. Two people who start as mates and continue as lifemates can eventually *grow* into soulmates.

"Yes," I offered. "Life is cyclical..." *Marriage is cyclical, too; or maybe more like a boomerang.* "You can't stay down forever. Something has to give. It's all going to work out."

"And what if it doesn't?"

"It will. But if it doesn't, then *I'll* get a job doing whatever I have to do for us."

He looked at me, knowing I meant it.

"Besides," I waxed on. "Health is wealth." ...*And there is always another bentonite clay cleanse and who knows what else is at the top of that hill if I keep climbing and aspiring to higher ideals?*

"No, it's not. It's just health."

Sense of humor: another double-edged sword of a trait I would add to the Jon section of my happiness list that I planned not only to keep growing but checking in with. Because while I was aspiring, I was also learning to touch down on a little planet called Reality from time to time.

"Everyone needs to understand that you can love somebody and still not like them once in a while."

 - *K.G., Locust Valley, married twenty-five years*

"The challenge is to evolve together."

 - *K.T., Roslyn, married nineteen years*

ABDICATION

We were at the movies on a Saturday night in July when he came back to me. It was through a small gesture, possibly unconscious—one that would doubtfully impress anyone else—but I noticed as I walked outside the restroom.

And found him waiting for me.

He'd always stood outside that door during our courtship period, of course, but at some point over the years, he'd taken to roaming the corridors of the theatre instead, checking his phone by the water fountains or pacing the sidewalk, getting air. And while I'd always been able to easily spot his curly dark head bobbing above the crowd, walking out and finding him waiting for me was way better.

Yes, I would be careful not to expect it from him, but that didn't mean I couldn't enjoy the bonus of a good thing when it happened. Kind of like experiencing the weather; my mood wouldn't be dependent on sunny days, but that didn't mean I couldn't revel in one.

"Hi," I said, darted by the romantic triangle tip that had been blunted for so long.

"Wait." He placed his hand on my shoulder and toed off a stray piece of toilet paper stuck to my sandal heel.

"Why, *thank you.*"

"Come on, you." He pulled me closer, then tucked my arm into the crook of his elbow and walked us toward the exit, the heat of his body radiating against me. "So what did you think of the movie?" he asked.

"The ending got me."

"Me too."

"And I wanted to love the rest. I mean—twelve years to film it? But I probably could have been just as happy if they'd shot it in two years and cast different actors to play the parts."

"I feel the exact same way. It definitely dragged in the middle somewhere."

We glided through the crowd, arm in arm, our love triangle intact, for the moment. While my definition of us and our roles had changed, I still believed it *was* possible to have eroticism, romance, and companionship within our marriage, even if it was a rare evening when they were happening all at once. Some days I knew only two points might sharpen, some months—or years—only one. In this way, love seemed as much like a vertebra in need of adjustments.

So, would I have drunk the poison right then and there?

In a way, I already had.

As to whether Jon would have downed that vial for me, I couldn't say, but it was around this time, that he did shock the hell out of me. I don't remember how we'd started talking about trains and cars, and jumping in front of them to save people—I think it had to do with a conversation with Eddie about self-driving cars and the debate on whether Google should program them to save the driver versus saving the public at large. In any case, Jon blurted out that he'd naturally jump in front of a car to save me. And I'd stood there, blinking in shock.

"What's your problem, Heather?"

"You really would?"

"Don't be ridiculous, of course I would," he'd said.

And I knew he was telling the truth.

Granted, he could have been saying this for Julia's benefit. And granted, his reasoning might have had its own utilitarianism—maybe he believed it better for our family at large if he took the hit. *The right way.*

He might also have been conjecturing—who knows what would happen in the actual moment. But while he wasn't saying, "I'd drink the poison because I can't live without you," he was offering protection—and no one had forced him at knifepoint to offer it. I'd take it.

"What's going on in that head of yours?" he asked as we walked past the concession stand, fragrant with buttered popcorn.

"Oh, nothing." He smiled and shook his head, and, like that, his gratitude felt palpable to me. Were we back to telepathy? I could practically hear his thoughts. *It was Saturday night. He was out with his wife. He had a companion in life. We were of one mind about the movie we'd just seen.*

There was a lot that hadn't been perfect between us through the years, but also a lot that had worked like a charm if we stopped to take the time to think about it—like our intellectual simpatico, and maybe even our general taste in all things cultural.

A girlfriend recently told me a story about her parents, how she'd called them on a Sunday at six p.m. and learned that she'd missed "the cut off period" to talk; her mother was "going up" for the night, and her father was "settled in" downstairs. This had become her parents' routine after fifty years of marriage, to part after dinner and watch their separate shows. It was a funny anecdote but scary. *At least,* I thought to myself, *we wouldn't be that.* But everyone had a different deal breaker, I was beginning to realize, and who knew what her parents' deal breaker was?

Though perhaps with a little effort, even the deal breakers could be worked through with the right mindset.

He stopped at the exit door of the theatre. I looked at

him. He waited. "Aren't you going to open it for me like a gentleman?" I asked.

"You won't touch that germ-infested door handle, will you?"

"Nope."

"I knew it!" He opened the door, chuckling, and I felt my heart swell.

Back to laughing about my idiosyncrasies instead of lambasting me for them. Wow. Maybe he was changing, too?

That a sense of mortality was setting in, probably helped the cause, too. That summer one of his contemporaries invited us to Pennsylvania for his wedding to wife number three and by connecting with all his friends, Jon caught up on everyone's breakdowns and diseases.

As Jon introduced me, holding my hand tightly, he seemed to show me off as if I were some kind of trophy wife.

"Your wife is beautiful," they all told him. Beautiful? Or *still ten years younger?*

Jon was flabbergasted at how different everyone seemed. One of his old buddies literally looked like a cartoon Santa. Julia wouldn't leave his side; I had to pry her away from the poor guy. Somehow, Jon had managed to age better.

"Must be all the good food I feed you—not to mention those green juices," I whispered to him as we lay in the hotel bed afterward, Julia snuggled between us. His one juice cooler had turned into a regular weekly thing, and he'd been downing wheatgrass for months like nobody's business.

"A calorie is a calorie, Heather. I've been eating less. Juicing isn't magic."

Wasn't it? He had lost twenty pounds and seemed lighter, easier, definitely less focused on correcting the small things. One night, after we'd cleaned up the kitchen, I'd returned to find him reorganizing my dishwasher work without a word of complaint. I was impressed! I went to him as he was bent over the machine and massaged his shoulders. "I am so, so proud of you," I said.

"Don't push your luck." But he was smiling.

Was he learning to appreciate? Even Julia had begun to have her suspicions.

"There are my girls," he boomed, walking into the den one afternoon. "What are my beautiful girls doing?"

She looked up from drawing and stared at him quizzically.

"Just saying hi before I head to the gym." He admired her work and kissed her forehead. "Okay, bye." He waved and turned on his sneaker heel.

"Is he going crazy or what?" She went back drawing.

I liked to think my own perspective was somehow acting as a mirror of change for him—a perspective that was incidentally shifting by the day and becoming more optimistic. I wouldn't dare tell Jon this, but I'd started taking an interest in more science-based reading. And it was in these texts at the bookstore that I found out some *positive* facts about marriage, like the fifty percent divorce rate we all tout so cavalierly is actually a number from the 1970s, and with each passing decade the divorce rate has actually been on the decline; or that only about *ten percent* of married couples are cheating on their spouses, despite what websites like *Ashley Madison* would have us believe; or that marriage has health benefits for all involved; or that studies show that kids thrive in a two-parent household (the caveat being that the relationship has to be good between these adults), and that married people are likelier to live a few years longer than their single counterparts.

It was likely, however, that Jon's own positive attitude stemmed from the progress he'd been making with work. That September he'd received a term sheet from a hotel company, signaling that his project was finally a go.

Maybe, too, a new cycle had begun.

The stores had started to do slightly better as well. They weren't going to make us rich anytime soon, but they were chugging along, meeting their bills and throwing us a few dollars now and then.

I had gotten some help. My brother-in-law, a marketing manager, stepped in with some ideas on how to grow the business. My cousin, a chef specializing in raw foods he called "Rowan's Originals"—though initially mystifying Massapequa, with "zucchini pasta lasagna," replete with walnut "meat"—kept the customers coming back for more. Also to join the team was "Organic Greg"—a health food store veteran by day, lead singer of *New York Dirt* by night— who actually knew the supposed uses of things like oregano oil and deer antler. Unlike a lot of health food store gurus I'd met before, he called bullshit. When people rushed in looking for the newest Dr. Oz suggestion, we sent them to Organic Greg who usually counseled them to eat better and exercise rather than rushing off to take green coffee-bean extract. While that wasn't perfect for sales, it did help develop a core philosophy. Borrowed from Hippocrates, we were all about "let[ting] thy food be thy medicine." As for those empty grocery shelves that had prompted people to ask if we had just opened or were closing, I took some down, and nudged the place into more of a juice bar/deli and less of a grocery-vitamin store. (Eventually, the store would turn into a restaurant).

At the beauty bar, my childhood friend decided to come aboard—eager to find her own lifeline and utilize her creativity. She was the type of person who'd always been able to wrap presents in grocery and garbage bags and still make them look good. Her first order of business was to chuck most of the makeup. Her second was to transform the store into a spa/boutique with pocketbooks, clothes, and jewelry—things my sister's clients seemed to actually want.

That store remained more of a struggle, but I'd started

to accept, as with my marriage, that I'd created this little world and dealing with its responsibilities and limitations, even when I didn't always feel like it, was part of the deal. Reminding myself that I wasn't a prisoner and could bail anytime I wanted helped my mindset, too.

Some days, I even enjoyed transforming women. Maybe it wasn't a high art form or my higher calling, but there was *some* value in helping a woman feel pretty—and in making her laugh. "No smiling allowed in this chair," I would say, "only misery allowed." And she would chuckle.

More important was learning to be happy without success—without attaching my self-worth to a label or a paycheck or a title.

If I would ever fully believe I had "succeeded"—having lost a lot of money and time trying to make a business profitable—was still in the works. But maybe it was *possible* that I had just chosen the wrong races to run.

That winter my skin stayed clear. Jon roamed the plains and leapt after the gazelles, proudly dragging them home and stockpiling their carcasses in the bank. I started to think about the long haul of marriage, how maybe there was something to be said for Harriet's remark about just sticking it out—to allow for the bad years in marriage to be replaced by more good years.

No, our story would not become the first-ever non-fiction tale of true love uninterrupted, after all. But we still had a chance to write the future. And more than ever, in a world climate of hostile tempers and intolerance, the love narrative—in all its forms and shapes, especially the unconditional love part of the narrative—seemed not a lofty ideal but a *necessary* one to perpetuate. The image of fireflies came to mind, lighting up across the world, and I thought if, just for the briefest of seconds a day, every household chose an act of love to supersede indifference or hate, just how beautiful the landscape would look with billions of lights puncturing through the darkest of spaces.

"Tell me the story of when you and Daddy got married," Julia asked me recently. As I began to tell her about Starbucks and visions of Mexico, and me stealing her daddy's bathing suit in the water and not being able to stop smiling when I looked at him, I was reminded of something I'd recently read about the way we view our marriages and the stories we tell. How we choose to tell them, and how we choose to remember them, shapes the present form of our relationships, as much as our history does.

Yes, there is a place for cynicism in these narratives—over tribal wine and coffee with our girlfriends as we check in with each other to laugh and keep it real. But for our children, and for our families, and most of all, for the health of our own hearts, it's important to preserve the positive narrative of love.

We took a vacation that February. There was a lot to feel good about. For things we didn't yet know—like that we would eventually sell our house, and this time *I* would find us a place, something smaller and full of farmhouse character for me, yet roomy enough to pacify Jon's ego; a house that Jon, former Mr. Ferguson Castle, would not only surprise me by loving but also by agreeing to furnish with shiplap. *Shiplap.* Moreover, the purchase would unfold in such a fortuitous way that Jon would look at me and say, "Maybe the Universe *did* conspire," and I would stand there, slack-jawed. But Chapter Five, entitled, *Did He Really Just Say That?* had yet to be written.

For the moment, we were simply grateful—for Jon to be happily working and for everyone's health and well-being. Emily had secured an upcoming internship at an architecture firm. Eddie was up to four employees at his tech start-up in San Francisco. Julia was thriving in the second grade, and I'd even found a small press to publish my manuscript into a book. Jon cried at the book launch—a bonus for me to see him so proud and overcome, just as it was to read Lorna's words of praise.

But the feeling *I'd done it* trumped all. And maybe, too, that I could keep doing it.

Writing, even as I was living.

Dear Heather,
Remember that ridiculous time when you tried to deter mice with those peppermint pouches?

Writing to discover and evolve.

We planned a drive up the coast of California. The weather cooperated. A friend told me that Los Angeles gets one balmy week in February. Whether it's true or not, it felt like lady luck was back on our side as the weather turned warm the week we landed.

In our T-shirts and flip-flops, we walked the obligatory Hollywood Boulevard and went to Grauman's Chinese Theatre, holding our breath over the smell of urine along the way and remarking how the place seemed reminiscent of Times Square in the 80s before anyone had cleaned it up. Jon was in a great mood, cracking jokes and looking for the humor in things—being next to him felt reminiscent of our earliest years.

We walked Rodeo Drive and let Julia believe, as she insisted, that she'd just seen Kim Kardashian dip into a jewelry store. We traipsed through the farmer's market, a glorified shopping mall, a.k.a. Jon's nightmare—a crowded shopping center where no one was in a hurry.

"My god," he said, weaving around slow walkers, though we had no real agenda. "How do people go through life?"

"We commoners eventually figure it out," I told him.

"Very funny," he said, still not the least bit apologetic about his remark.

We headed out of the city, stopping in Santa Barbara to

rendezvous with Eddie at a Thai restaurant. He immediately noticed the change in his dad.

"Do I know this guy?" he said when Jon was out of earshot.

The next day, we took in Big Sur, one of the most magnificent places on Earth, though I resisted suggesting we move there or anywhere. It's not so much that I'd made peace with Long Island as much as I'd decided that the geography of the self mattered more. The rest was just scenery.

Jon, of course, would have begged to differ.

Winding around the ledge of a mountain with a drop of at least two hundred feet, below which was the sea and craggy rocks, gave him a major anxiety attack. It was a tall person thing. Or maybe just a Jon thing, as Eddie—who was now six-foot-seven—seemed to have no problem with the rails ending mid-calf. But even Jon's anxiety attack was manageable—and laughable. He'd stopped in the restroom to deal with the "adrenaline dump," and returned looking pale but tickled.

"I feel pretty light in my loafers," he said.

"If you think about it," I said, "it doesn't actually make sense that nature would build in the need to evacuate as a flight or fight response. You can run faster with your bowels emptied, but you have to factor in the time it takes to pull down your pants and squat."

"Maybe it's to create a slip and slide for the lions and tigers chasing you," Jon said.

"Nature's banana peel," Eddie said.

"I'm going to throw up now," Julia said.

We arrived in Carmel and were making dinner plans for Clint Eastwood's Mission Ranch, where I was excited to see sheep roaming the field and hoped there wouldn't be lamb chops on the menu, when the call came in. Jon hung up and sighed. Two investors were backing out and another was on the fence.

"It's just a temporary setback," I said, rubbing his back.

"I hope so," he said.

Eddie threw me a look. "I'm going to go get ready," he said.

"Good idea. Meet you in twenty."

We went back to our rooms to shower. I was braiding Julia's hair when Jon stepped out. With a towel wrapped around his waist, he held something small and rectangular in his hand. "Heath? What is this?"

From across the room, I squinted. "Deodorant?"

"Kiss my Face? Lavender and chamomile? Did you really pay $8.99 for this?"

Oh, geez, I could practically feel my skin begin to tingle. Was the boomerang slinging outward again, and so soon?

Deep breaths.

The happiness list...and maybe some of those new ideas I'd been thinking about lately. Brick and mortar stores were out, that was for sure. But some of those other things that dropped into my brain, were they not Shark Tank worthy?

Maybe. Although I wasn't quite sure which of the two was the more marketable yet—Clean Feet, an ionizing welcome mat that sanitized the bottom of shoes or the Headache Buster, an acupressure pointer for the soft cushion between the thumb and forefinger.

Of course I would need to sketch out my business plan before I entered the Open Casting Call...

Or maybe it would be better to wing it.

More From the Tribe:

"When you get married before you know yourself, it's not a good thing."

- *M.M., Massapequa, married fourteen years*

"We weren't meant to stay together this long. We were supposed to die in our teens. Modern medicine ruined everything."

- *J.M., Deer Park, married fourteen years*

"If things are within the happy to somewhat tolerable range 50% of the time then you're doing well."

- *D.S., Nesconset, married eight years*

"You should know going in that you will wind up hating that person. Especially after children, you will hate them the most. But don't give up."

- *C.W., married fifteen years*

"Three things we all need to be happy: work, love, and connection."

- *M.G., marriage therapist*

"Always kiss each other goodnight."

- *K.L., married fourteen years*

"Never tell them how much you REALLY spent on something."

- *S.F., Northport, married twenty-one years*

"I love my second husband a lot, and I think our

relationship is successful because I find him sexy."
  - J., Rockville Centre, married six years

"Be friends. Don't make it all about sex. Be with someone you want to have a conversation with."
  - J.P., Merrick, widow, married for twenty-one years

"Sex is paramount to the relationship. When the times get hard, it's often this connection that will re-establish the intimate bond you feel with your mate."
  - H.F., Merrick, married sixteen years

"There's no such thing as fair. You should try and stick with the things you're good at and be prepared to do the things that you're not so good at. Some weeks I'm not so good at anything. That's why blow jobs were invented."
  - Anonymous

"Marriage is work, but so is life! Waking up to the same person everyday knowing you have a partner to go through the good, the bad and the evil with is comforting. Working through the tough times and conquering them brings you to a deeper level of love and gratitude each time."
  - T.T., formerly from Bellmore, married twenty-three years

"Being a modern feminist means doing what you want on your own terms."
  - P. J. Wantagh, married eleven years

"People say they wouldn't change a thing. I would change everything."
  - J.P., North Bellmore, married sixteen years
"It's true that I wouldn't have had my kids if I hadn't married him. But I would have had other kids!"
  - D.M. Commack, married seventeen years

"Remember what made you say yes."
- *M.I., married thirteen years*

"You have to have a big heart and a lot of forgiveness."
- *Anonymous*

"People don't take enough time to find their person before marriage."
- *S.B., married fourteen years*

"Everyone's on something on Long Island. The problem with drinking is that when you wake up, you're still with the same person."
- *Anonymous*

"You need to find someone who loves you more than you love them."
- *K.L., married fourteen years*

"Marry someone you respect."
- *K.B., married twelve years*

"Get married once before you actually get married for real."
- *J.O., married thirteen years*

"I say I'm sorry for the things I'm not sorry for all the time."
- *C.M. Glen Cove, married three years*

"Listen to each other. Not the words. But to what the person is saying."
- *M.M., married thirteen years*

"Sometimes keep your mouth shut. But not always."

- S.L., married fifty years

"If Long Island had more places to go and things to do, maybe we wouldn't feel so pent up."
- Anonymous

"Kiss hello and goodbye every day."
- J.S. Seaford, married seven years

Things We Tell Our Kids Before They Leave the House:

"Have courage and be brave."
"Make good choices."
"Be gentle in your actions and stay safe."
"No biting."
"Don't be an asshole."
"Please put a poopie in the potty today."

Things We Say Behind Our Kids' Backs:

"Be their biggest advocate."
"Teach them to be who they are."
"Always have their back."
"Make alone time for each of your kids."
"Teach them if they accept the invitation, to make sure their presence is value-added."
Allow your kids to be authentically who they are and love them for it."
"Take others' parenting opinions with a grain of salt."
"Always keep a nail clipper in the car."

For more follow @heather_siegel